## THE INNER DOMINATRIX GUIDE:

# BECOME A BADASS
# IN BUSINESS

Dana Pharant

The Inner Dominatrix Guide: Become A Badass In Business

**ISBN** 978-1-9994610-0-3

**Photo Credits:** Selina Photography

**Cover Design:** Andjela Vujic

**Editor:** Aprille Janes

Connect with Dana

http://danapharant.com

dana@danapharant.com

"Live with anything long enough

every blessing will become a curse, and

every curse will become a blessing"

Time has an incredible ability to change how we view our lives and others - the longer we live with a problem, the less of an issue we think it is. That is until it is removed. Then we begin to discover the full extent of impact that it really had on our lives and psyche.

This realization came when I chose to step into the dungeon, journeying into an adventure, only to find the most unexpected healing.

# INTRODUCTION

For some, business is a means to an end, and then there are the wild and crazy people like me who dive into business as if it were an extreme sport. Using business as a way to challenge me to grow and expand as a human being with each new challenge. Each new level has required me to dig deeper and show up more authentically.

I love to bring my dedication to my spiritual growth and consciousness into all that I do, from Kink to Business. Blending all of my passions into one book has not been an easy task and one that I have taken on with you the reader in mind with each word I typed.

I hope you find the stories engaging, and even more, I hope that you make use of the tools presented in this book to expand who you are personally, professionally and spiritually so that you can really step into Being a Badass in Business.

Being a badass is not about being hard and callus, but rather it is an embracing of the masculine and feminine energy within each of us so that we can access the gifts that come from each of these energies. Cheers!

Dana Pharant

# What others are saying
# about this book

"*Dana Pharant manages a wonderfully fine balance of combining a sense of fun and irreverancy with proven grounded self-improvement processes that have worked for her many clients, making for a uniquely entertaining, insightful, powerful and inspiring read. I walked away from this book feeling empowered, enlightened and just a little more badass in my own approach to business and to life.*"

Mark Leslie Lefebvre - Writer
Bookseller, POD & eBook Keener, Book Nerd
https://starkreflections.ca

"*Dana's work was instrumental in moving me out of overwhelm, letting go of running my business from the draining push energy for a more fulfilling and successful business. I love how she has brought so much of her story and her gifted tools into this book.*"

Odette Peek
Soul Story Strategist
http://odettepeek.com/

"*Dana shares a unique perspective that allows any business owner or entrepreneur to step into their greatest power with both courage and authentic grace, UNapologetically. This is a must read if you want you to get your message out into the world in a way that will create positive transformation for millions.*"

Davide Di Giorgio
Speaker and International Best Selling Author of *Being Unapologetic*
www.DavideSpeaks.com


*"Dana's transformation from her experience in a cult, to becoming a badass in business is nothing short of inspirational. Her raw, real and honest approach to guiding you towards a deeper truth about your limitlessness may not be what you expect - but may be exactly what you need!"*

Codi Shewan
Keynote Speaker, Trainer, Consultant
www.CODISHEWAN.com


*"There are a lot of coaches out there who help you to break through to the next level, but with Dana, she brings in an unlikely yet profoundly dynamic approach - the power of the Dominatrix.*

*My life has radically shifted as a result of both Dana's coaching and this book. I have been able to drop into a soft feminine power that allows me to feel as strong as mother earth and to create universes in record time.*

*Since working with Dana the drama in my life has gone to zero, my income has quadrupled, and my ability to manifest has become like magic this book is a must-read."*

Cindy Ashton
Singer, Performance Coach, TV Host and more
www.cindyashton.com

# Table of Contents

# Foreword

From her childhood in the Church to the depths of the dungeon, Dana takes us on a journey to understand how past traumas and beliefs hold us back from stepping into our magnificence. Embracing the principles of the Inner Dominatrix energy, we're emboldened to accept what we desire, reject that which doesn't serve us, and to create opportunities that are greater than we believed possible.

This guide will challenge you to let go of deeply held beliefs that are comfortably rooted in your brain so that you can be more, do more and, most importantly, feel more with ease and badass confidence.

As a CEO and tech start-up founder, I've struggled with balancing all aspects of my life. Being married to my co-founder doesn't help – hard conversations about company business doesn't make for sexy pillow talk. What I've discovered by working with Dana and channeling my Inner Dominatrix is that I'm no longer making apologies for my needs and desires – personally or professionally.

Doing the work to clear our emotional baggage takes practice. This guide has great tools to revisit to clear out the noise – the "who do you think you are," "what makes you think you deserve this great promotion/relationship/bank balance?" Letting go of our past traumas means we can fly higher and achieve our goals. Getting to do it with your Dominatrix boots is that much more fun.

The world is waiting for you to step into your Inner Dominatrix. What are you waiting for?

Jean Leggett, CEO & Founder

One More Story Games

# Helpful Definitions

In writing this book, I am aware many will be drawn in by the title and the word *Dominatrix*. Given the millions of copies of 50 Shades of Grey that were sold, I am acutely aware the subjects of Kink and BDSM hold an allure for many, even if only as a fantasy.

Intrigued as you may be, there are terms used in this book which you may not have heard before. They are common terms to anyone actively involved in the Kink world, but I would do you, the reader, a disservice to assume you know these terms, so this is your quick guide.

**Kink** - A term used by those involved in BDSM to refer to BDSM-related activities. Your kink is anything outside of the typical sexual experience. 'Typical' is often what you would think good 50's household married couple participating in. We know in reality there is no such thing as typical. It can range from sensual to all out hard core pain, from any number of dress-up costume play to role play fantasy. There are as many kinks as there are people on this vastly different planet.

**BDSM** - Bondage & Discipline/Domination & Submission/Sadism & Masochism

**Scene** - When two people get together to engage in BDSM, it is called a scene. Not all BDSM involves sex, so a new term was created in place of hooking up or having sex.

This can also be referenced as playing - adult play, mind you.

**Dominatrix** - Generally refers to a woman who takes on submissive clients for a fee. Also referred to as a Pro-Domme. The term Dominatrix is also used even by those who do not receive pay. The vast majority of Pro-Dommes DO NOT have sexual contact with their clients so not a Pro-Domme is not a prostitute with a whip.

**Domme** - The same as Dominatrix, although some will opt for this term if they only engage for their own enjoyment and not for money. Personally, I prefer the term Dominatrix because it more clearly defines a woman, as opposed to Dom, which is the male version of the same role. Dom and Domme sound alike so why not go with something clearly different?

**Submissive** - One who enjoys surrendering their power and will to a Dom/Domme/Dominatrix.

**Sub-Space** - The "high" that can come as a result of surrendering into a kink scene. It is a spiritual high resulting from the mix of pleasure and pain and subsequent release of endorphins over a prolonged period of time (at least an hour). By slowly ramping up the intensity of pain, mixed with the exhilaration of the moment, the experience leads to this intensely meditative, out-of-body sensation that is also a deeply grounded moment. It's a place, where time and space cease to exist and you are only in the nanoseconds of NOW.

**Judgement** – While not a Kink term, I do want to clearly define how I am using the word in the context of this book. Some use this word to speak of discernment, but for this book, it has to do with the heavier type of judging yourself or others to be right or wrong, or good or bad that ends up creating emotional charges in our systems.

# Chapter 1

# MY STORY

When I started speaking at events and conferences, I was floored by the number of people who longed to hear more of my story. They came up after my presentations to ask if my first book covered this or where they could find out the rest of the story.

I will admit I had no intention of going into great depth about my story when I wrote this book but after repeated requests here it is.

Until I was 18 I lived in a mild religious cult with a family who bought it hook, line and sinker.

I grew up in the home of an Elder (church leader) in the Jehovah Witness religion. This organization does an outstanding job of keeping its disciples insulated among its own kind, which is one of the prominent markers making this religion more of a cult than an organization or belief system.

While I did go to school with kids not of this religion, I wasn't allowed to socialize with them outside of school. In high school, I purposely sought out the nerdy girls to hang out with. While I got along with everyone, I was more comfortable with the geeky, unpopular group. They weren't judgemental, and they never had parties I had to say no to. It was just easier that way.

As a result, I failed to develop any kind of deep friendships at school so when I chose to walk away from the religion at 18, I walked away from all my family, community and friends. I did not have much built up in the way of outside support beyond that circle to help me through this experience.

I moved out of this extremely strict religious household and moved in with my birth mother. Her home was the extreme opposite of the home I'd left behind. Here there were free-flowing drugs, alcohol and sex.

It was as if I landed on a planet devoid of gravity, suddenly floating free, without boundaries or a sense of what was okay or not okay. Anything I wanted to try was an option, which sounds great as a teen, but in honesty, it left me lost and grasping at air. Nothing to land my feet solidly on and say, "This is me."

The choice to leave my father's home wasn't simple or easy. I had been dying inside a little more each day by staying. His religion felt so utterly out of alignment with who I was inside. I had no words for that tiny spark deep inside except that I felt a pull to stand tall in the world, to have people see me, and to make a difference.

I had no idea how to do that or even how to articulate what I felt. All I had then was this overwhelming push to get OUT! Eventually, who I longed to become surpassed any fears I had about leaving so out I went into the unknown world.

Recently, while researching and digging deeper into cults, their effects and how we break free of them, I stumbled across something interesting. Those who join cults lose their sense of identity and take on the thoughts and beliefs of these factions out of a necessity to fit in and sometimes in order to survive.

For me, I took on the idea that women were second class to men and were there for the pleasure and service of men. This was preached from the stage and modelled in the hierarchy of who was allowed to lead.

Also profoundly embedded in me was this impossible-to-reach ideal of not making "too much money," when "too much" was never defined. However, the most intriguing part for me in my research was when cult survivors finally break free, they gradually return to who they were before joining.

Having grown up in this cult, I had no other identity formed, so I had nothing to return to. Instead, I see in hindsight, that for the next 20 years I tried on the extremes of just about everything out there. I sampled a spectrum of ideas and ways of life until I found the balance point that worked for me.

I tried out alcohol and drugs for a while. I tried abstinence for a while. Eventually, I found a balance point of enjoying alcohol without using it to run away from my emotions or painful situations.

I sampled from the wide variety of self-help and self-improvement programs, diving headlong in, then jumping out and denouncing methods only to later pull some of it back in when I had found a happy medium that worked for me.

I spent many years attending groups like Al-Anon or ACA (Adult Children of Alcoholics), which were helpful in gaining clarity on why I was feeling fucked up. At the same time, the programs kept me telling the same story over and over, locking me into my story and victim status.

I also dove headlong into a modality called Access Consciousness, and while it gave me gifts in unlocking things at an energetic level that I had not been able to get to before, it too, was a mixed blessing. The further up I climbed up the learning ladder and title status, the more I saw how insane and dysfunctional the leaders and their system was.

At first, Access Consciousness gave me untold freedoms by unlocking my body energetically. Then it became like an abusive boyfriend who loved me deeply at first, showering me with gifts until eventually telling me I was crazy. If I was the broken one and he was perfect, I should adore him.

Thankfully I broke free of that interesting mess, too.

I did the extreme thing with food, too, taking on new eating regimes, going full out, then moving on to another. I embraced raw food with a passion. I juiced with gusto, and then sugar binged like a rock star.

You name it, I tried it.

From the outside, this looked really crazy. It wasn't until I read that information about returning to who you are after you leave a cult that it clicked for me. I needed to try out the extremes and have a contrast in experiences to see what worked for me.

At 19, I signed up at the local massage therapy college and spent the next two years learning way more about the human body than one would possibly think necessary to become a Massage Therapist. I recall sitting in Neurology class, suspecting I had gotten my classes mixed up and that

I was in the program for neurosurgeons instead of neurology for massage therapists.

Despite the incredible depth of our schooling, there was still a lot to be learned afterwards. No one talked much about energy work or the emotions of clients. Instead, we were told they were out of the scope of a massage practice and to just stick to the tools of our training.

Being the rebel I am, I ignored their advice and over the years studied in depth about energy and energy-based psychotherapy tools.

I noticed how intertwined a client's emotional state was to their physical state. I observed how when they would let go of the emotions attached to things, the muscles also released.

I worked with one client who suffered lower back pain for years. They went to yoga, chiropractic, and four other massage therapists before me, with little or no lasting change. Sure the problem lay in the energy/emotional system (it feels different than a physical disruption), I asked questions as I massaged. I moved the energy block by inviting them to talk about the money stress going on in their life. The more they talked, the more the muscles relaxed. By the end of that session, the back pain was gone for the first time in years.

Beating on the muscles until they let go was an ineffective use of my time, so I coached my clients through an emotional release. The physical complaint also shifted.

While I was quite likely viewed as practicing 'out of the scope of practice,' I earned a reputation for resolving problems no one else had been able to get a handle on for the clients. By testing out tools and seeing what worked repeatedly, I began the evolution of my work into the coaching model I use today.

While I was a massage therapist, I had one client who remains a dear friend. On her first visit, she disclosed she was actively involved in Kink, and there would be times she would have bruises. Anne wanted me to know so that she could talk honestly about where they were from and not have to make up a cover story. She told me so I would not be concerned she was being abused.

The way she disclosed and how she was clearly enthralled by this lifestyle intrigued me. I wanted to know more.

I secretly fantasized about having sex while being handcuffed or tied up, trying out these very kinds of things but I kept pushing them out of my mind. After all, they must have been some crazy, warped way my subconscious worked out the abuse I had gone through. Right?

Each time Anne came in, I asked a few more questions about Kink. Each time Anne openly shared with me in a way that was free of shame. We could have been talking about fine wine.

She loaned me books. One my favourite from those early days was *Screw the Roses; Send Me the Thorns* by Molly Devon and Philip Miller. A very comprehensive straight talk on how to add S&M into your life in a safe, sane, consensual way. I might have kept this book for a little too long, devouring a little more each night. Savouring the delicious ideas and dreaming of the day when I could try them out.

Actually adding it to my life was left to fantasy land for the most part. The partner I lived with at the time was not really keen on it. Because he was submissive, he was not much help to me in exploring my own submissive side.

Eventually, I gave up my need to change him and left, opening my world to Kink. I went to parties, joined Fet-Life (a Kink version of Facebook), and social gatherings. I had tea with other kinky people and attended as many workshops as I could.

It became my world outside of work. A society that changed me in more ways than I could have imagined.

For my first party, I went with Anne and her husband and met some more friends there. Anne and her friends kept an eye on me - a common practice in the Kink community for newbies. I went in thinking I was just going to observe, 'check things out.' That lasted all of an hour before I was sitting on the couch with handcuffs.

"Just observing, I see," called one of my new friends keeping watch, throwing me a wink.

Once in, it is pretty hard not to be all in so by the second hour, I was up on one of the spanking benches, having my first kink experience and hitting the incredible high known as 'sub-space,' that place where time stops and nothing else exists. I still laugh at a moment after my 'scene.' A fellow partygoer came up to me to say how much he loved watching the two of us play and that I had a nice ass.

Suddenly, the illusion that the scene was just my Dom and me was shattered. The awareness that I was not alone and my whole experience was on public display came crashing down on me. During the scene, I had been completely lost in the moment, and the only thing that existed for me was my partner and me as if we were the only two people on the planet. It jarred me, to say the least, to find out my private island was not so private after all. It is incredible the tricks the mind can play on you at times.

And yet despite my moment of awareness of being on display, the high was far greater than I could have hoped or imagined. It left me with an even greater desire to experience more.

These 'scenes,' as they are referred to in the Kink world, opened me up to see just how strong I was. I discovered a hidden ability to surrender deeply and be transformed.

I also felt fortunate to connect with someone who had a natural talent for healing and brought that energy to his scenes. His intentional awareness of the energy component of kinky play allowed my body to release the trauma.

You see, trauma is stored on an energetic level in the system so, naturally, that is also how we unlock it – with energy tools. Through our private sessions together I released years of trauma and abuse from my body in a way I had not realized I needed. My pelvic area became more mobile, and my orgasms were stronger and more easily reached. And those were just a couple of the changes I experienced.

Only when the walls were gone did I realize just how much energy I used to hold them and keep others at a safe distance. I finally made the connection between the lifetime of depression and the residual abuse stored physically and energetically in my cells, just waiting to be released.

Trauma, such as a sexual assault, sets up a "program" that negatively affects the body. Our bodies have a mechanism which controls the "stress response." When we encounter a trauma and it is not addressed or resolved, then our bodies become disrupted. We can get stuck in the loop of pumping out adrenaline and cortisol which in turn affects the rest of the body and eventually becomes a severe adrenal burnout.

Instead of the body hitting a reset after the trauma, it loops over and over into low-grade panic mode. This low-grade panic mode and constant cortisol pumping into the system is directly linked to dysfunctions of the endocrine system, depression, and a suppressed immune system. The loop can effectively be interrupted and brought back into harmony with an energetic release of the disrupting force (the trauma that is stuck energetically and its energetic programs).

My surrender into the submissive role and re-creating the scenes from my abuse with an outcome that left me feeling empowered and more connected to my body, allowed me to break the energetic programs trauma had set up. The programs kept me on high alert all the time which perpetually triggered the release of adrenaline and cortisol. Cutting these programs allowed me to relax again and calmed my nervous system. The depression lifted, and my sense of well-being returned. My magical healing journey through this most unexpected source gave me a longing to try out the other side of the whip. I wanted to be the one to take people on this tour and unlock the mysteries held within.

I picked up an assortment of tools of the trade - every new venture begins with some shopping after all - and I ventured into learning the skills of the Dominatrix. I bought beautiful custom lightweight whips with flexible handles that would not strain my wrists; white leather wrist and ankle cuffs – matching of course; some paddles, riding crops and suspension gear, to name just a few of the goodies in my adult toy box.

This adventure challenged me to grow and stretch personally in ways I never imagined. Learning to call someone degrading names was utterly out of my comfort zone but what they requested and desired pushed me to set aside my pre-conceived ideas to show up for the person in front of me.

Who I became to successfully pull off a convincing scene seemed to re-write my very DNA. I stepped into this persona of the Dominatrix, a woman who took charge, bossed people around for their own good and never apologized (during the scene at least).

I couldn't just pretend because the distinct energy from someone who owns that they are in charge is radically different compared to someone who fakes it. Many submissives will only surrender to a Domme who is really steeped in that energy. I had to become her.

It spilled over into my work and how I ran my business. I no longer let customers make unreasonable demands of my staff and me. I fired clients who disrespected me and allowed myself to take time off.

This Inner Dominatrix energy was vitally needed since I had not been running my business effectively. I hired people who needed jobs instead of hiring those who were a good fit for the position. This, of course, led to mistakes in orders and shipping which cost me money at every turn. In fact, my million-dollar business teetered on the brink of bankruptcy.

Bringing in my Dominatrix energy made all the difference.

That energy brought a stronger leadership to the helm and, although bankruptcy was unavoidable due to a series of unfortunate losses in the final months, I navigated those rough waters and turned the loss into something beneficial.

I was fully willing to lose the business to build it back up in a way that worked for me instead of attempting to make everyone else happy. I let go of having set hours for my store, took time off, and found creative solutions - like a partnership with another store to share a kiosk outlet while I went to Australia for two weeks.

During this transition, I noticed over and over that when I owned the Dominatrix energy (to show up unapologetically, to serve deeply without compromising, and to acknowledge my level of knowledge and skills), sales went up. When I let that energy slide, sales went down and customer complaints crept in. The pattern was as clear as turning a light on or off.

The more I experimented with this Inner Dominatrix energy in my business, the more I clarified the value of the teachings of the Dominatrix for business. I allowed that quiet confidence to ooze out of my pores for each client and supplier as we interacted. They walked away standing a bit taller as a result.

I said "No" without any explanation or justification, which eliminated or reduced discussions and arguments from customers. I offered valuable up-sells with zero attachment to the outcome, knowing it was in their best interest. Roughly 70% of the time, they happily said yes and many of these customers thanked me for the recommendation the next time they were in.

I began to see exactly how these skills and mindset were not only transferable but vital for anyone running a company, regardless of the niche or size. Thus began my quest to bring the Dominatrix Guide to Inner Power in Business to the world.

# Chapter 2

# WHERE IT ALL BEGAN

There are some things you live with for so long that you fail to even consider they might be a problem. There are things that, until they are removed, you would have sworn did not affect you.

For me, it was sexual trauma. Intellectually I had come to terms with it yet still it festered in my body. At least it did before I stepped into the world of Kink.

I had grown accustomed to feeling dull, uptight, and hyper-vigilant no matter who I was with or what I was doing. Always on high alert, I was aware of what everyone was doing, thinking and feeling.

While I pretended those skills were required for my job as a healer, I felt perpetually cut off from myself and others. I had long forgotten what it felt like to relax and feel alive in my body. I would even say I assumed it wasn't possible and I should just suffer like a good martyr. After all, that was modelled for me many times as the right course of action.

Those early experiences in the Kink world showed me what I had stuffed deep into the closets of my soul.

Tapping into those long silent voices gave them permission to rise again and sing out as I surrendered to the thud of the flogger on my back. To release the demons trapped in my body, I fought against the restraints on my wrists and wept openly at the most intimate moments of the scene. I took back what had been stolen all those years before. To be allowed to feel powerlessness in the presence of someone that I knew to be kind and loving; I screamed all the screams that had been unexpressed - not allowed as a teen. I could release all the 'no's' that had been stuffed down into my body. At the end of the scene, I was held, accepted for all that I saw as ugly, seen at the core of my being, and still loved. This allowance of ALL of me was the foundation of the healing. The space of the scene allowed me to explore the darker emotions, going back in time and letting them out, and most importantly the scene held a space for me to allow love, forgiveness and transformation in the end. Bringing closure in a way that would also allow me to experience gratitude for the experiences of the past.

After several sessions in the hands of gifted Doms, my body released and unwound the trauma in a way I never imagined possible. I relaxed for the first time in years. I felt a joy that had seemed ever elusive. I finally saw the wonder of the world and the beauty in all aspects of life. The grey skies filled with drizzly rain, the endless traffic jams, the challenges of day-to-day life suddenly had a charm and grace woven into the mess and chaos.

I was hooked.

I wanted more.

I needed more.

I signed up for any party within 200 miles. I scoured for events and play partners to experience more. I let my work slide and put off business meetings. I became obsessed. I spent my off hours reading about Kink or at play parties.

This world offered freedom and healing for me so I may have gone off the deep end, perhaps even a little OCD but that is my style. All or nothing.

As my sexual trauma healed, I came alive and discovered what desire was. Of course, at that point, my desire was channelled into the Kink world, regardless of where I focused that passion. It had been let out of the bottle. There was no turning back.

I later discovered a deeper layer of this sexual trauma to untangle, but at that time, the transformation was incredible. I itched to be able to give that transformation to others. I moved to the other side of the whip, playing with the energy as well as the physical props of Kink. I took people through an incredible healing journey, freeing up their bodies and reconnecting them with desire and passion while untangling the old wounds and hurts.

Each thud of the flogger pounded out traumas locked up in their bodies. Each crack of the whip took them deeper, releasing the past and reconnecting with the present. Moving with the energy in a rhythmical dance, casting a trance on the submissive, it took them to a place of surrender.

Sweet surrender releases past and present stresses. Surrender demands you to be fully present and convinces you that only this moment exists. When time and space disappear, the only awareness you have is the small circle that includes you and your Domme.

As you come down from the sub-space bliss, the effects of the release remain. The stress of the world has been removed for a day or two, maybe even as long as two weeks.

You feel grounded and centred as you move about your day-to-day activities. You calmly take on the most significant challenges as a result of dropping all the stress and baggage from your body.

This grounded-ness and peace keeps people coming back for more, time and again. If you have never experienced Kink, imagine the best massage you have ever had and multiply it by at least 20. That comes close to the experience of a really good session.

There is nothing else quite like it.

Not everyone feels the pull to experience the deep surrender of a session with a Dominatrix nor do they need to. There are many ways to get to the same blissed-out energy, many paths to deep re-connection with self.

Pick one that calls to you and dive in with reckless abandon. If you are even a tiny bit like me, once you get a taste of freedom from the baggage and trauma stored in your cells, you will want more.

You will want more not because you are broken or need to be fixed but rather, out of a desire to see the range and extent of what is possible. Your curiosity is aroused, and you long for a deeper connection to yourself. Just because it feels so incredible.

If you have experienced sexual trauma, it is essential to engage in healing in a way that releases the trauma from your body. You must unwind and unravel the hold it has on you to be genuinely free and stand in your power.

This is one area I strongly encourage people to seek a professional to take you through the process. Being therapist and patient at the same time through an area filled with emotional landmines invites disaster. Allowing someone to help who is trustworthy and has your back is all part of the healing process.

Even if you have done the base level work, I still urge you to work with someone skilled at untangling people from their trauma on a deep level. Otherwise, you may get to a point of functioning and think "I'm good, I don't need to go deeper." A good therapist or trauma coach will take you deeper, uprooting layers preventing you from feeling fully alive and at ease in your body.

Finally, a word for those who have been fortunate enough to have avoided a personal experience of abuse. Be aware that this kind of trauma can be passed on through generations. Energetically we take on the imprint of our parents. We can't help but be affected by them as we are strongly connected at an early and impressionable age. I have worked with clients who I would have sworn were sexually abused based on their energy, the way they carried themselves and the vocal constraints they exhibited. Yet when questioned, they would tell me they often get asked that while there was no trauma to them personally.

There have been some interesting studies done on the survivors of the Holocaust and their offspring, showing how the stress responses are altered in the children. Time will tell how this story unfolds in the generations to come, but for now, it is fascinating.

So even if you weren't abused, explore this area to see if there is value in deep trauma release for you as well.

## Success Stories!

*I couldn't remember a time when I didn't think about, plot and rage about getting revenge. Just for that one person who ripped my life apart when I was 17. I'm 61 now so you can imagine how much time I've wasted on this person. It affected every aspect of my life in many ways. Lack of confidence, self-esteem, sense of belonging, self-belief. You name it, it was damaged; I thought beyond repair, if I thought about it at all. Mostly, I cried, talked, whined, looked for solace in different addictions and sank into victimhood for many, many years.*

*Once I began my walk towards healing, I looked at everybody and what they were offering. There were a lot of people I took a pass on because what they offered just didn't ring true to me. Now as I look back, I can see that I didn't believe I was capable of the change I knew was needed. It was all part of the trauma I carried. I was stuck, blocked by fear, unable to admit to myself that I was terrified of change. Because I didn't know what would be on the other side.*

*Then I met Dana Pharant who offered her Inner Dominatrix work. It took a while for me to feel comfortable with her because of my many fears and blocks. As I attended groups at her home and different opportunities she offered, I began to use the tools she talked about. To expand out is a great one. I can feel myself grow in personal strength and confidence. It instantly puts me in my own power and practice perfects the feeling.*

*I've been working with Dana since January 2018 and I knew within two weeks that things were happening. I realized that the constant burning in my heart for revenge was gone. Completely and totally gone. I've tested myself, attempting to recall for a moment what it felt like, and it is completely gone. This and other things have caused me to feel that I am standing completely in my own power. This is an incredible feeling! There are residual quivers that require more work, however, it is totally manageable now. When I feel myself falter, I immediately expand and ground and if necessary, I repeat a mantra Dana gave me and I'm immediately back in my body. Things are moving so quickly now that it is even rare for that to be necessary.*

*My sense of personal power, strength, confidence and belonging is totally different now and I will never be the victim I thought I was. Things happened to me just like they have for others, but I've dealt with a lot of it and I can tell you I am in control of how I go forward from this place.*

~Jessie        Brandon        www.jessiebrandon.ca

# Chapter 3

# YES OR NO! SCREW THE MAYBE!

The Dominatrix is known for being strong, firm and decisive. She does not hesitate to state what she needs and directs things to work for her.

When you have submissives and slaves who long to be dominated, being wishy-washy is not going to cut it. They come to you to be able to hand over control. They want to believe in your power so they can surrender theirs for the session and experience the bliss to come.

You make a decision and direct your submissive to take action. Then, when you change your mind, you just tell them to take the new action.

Should your submissive choose to question you, it gives you a chance to implement "punishment" for being a mouthy little subby. Of course, this is a dance. We know the submissive looks for this "punishment," and it is part of the game. It is not actually punishment just as you are not genuinely angry with them, but we pretend in order to make the game more fun for everyone.

In the world of business, implementing punishment may need to be restricted to the secret world within your mind. However, the decisiveness of the Dominatrix is a trait we would all do well to emulate. Training yourself to be decisive is a process. It is a learned skill that, combined with the willingness to lose, propels your business forward.

In my research of how long CEOs take to make decisions, I discovered that those studied make 50% of their decisions in an average of just 9 minutes once they have all the information. So, too, the Dominatrix needs to make choices quickly and without hesitation.

During the summer of 2012 when I went through my business restructuring, I had so many decisions to make every day and so many things needing to be done that the luxury of time to deliberate or debate my options simply did not exist.

I had to move from 3600 sq. ft. to just 1200 sq. ft. This required me to sell off merchandise, racking, equipment, etc., all the while figuring out what needed to stay to make my new, smaller space work for me. Meanwhile, I also juggled all the paperwork, sales calls, website changes, and creditor calls while trying to stay sane.

Occasionally I even had time to eat.

This chaos was a tremendous gift to me. I learned to make decisions surprisingly quickly. In fact, I made choices in five to ten seconds on average. My previous practice of choosing based on the knowing of my gut-brain had accidentally trained me for this marathon. The practice of trusting my gut-brain became a test of my tools for a number of years. As a result, I felt uniquely positioned because I was connected to my intuition.

Given that I could not find a single instance in which my gut-brain was ever wrong, I now leaned on it for wisdom and guidance. There was zero time for any other option. Each choice was a "do or die moment."

Did all the decisions turn out well? Hell no!

Some were a mess, but I kept moving forward. Overall, things turned out for me better than I expected. Who is to say they didn't turn out well in the end? Sometimes we need to make a mess before we can re-arrange the pieces and create a masterpiece out of the disaster.

For example, when I made the choice to put my sinking Titanic of a business up for sale, the fallout eventually guided me to keep the store in a smaller, more manageable format. It turned out well for me even though at the time it felt like hell.

The choice to sell was chaotic. The first buyer was all gung-ho and had the money but the day before we were to close he got cold feet and pulled the plug. This left me scrambling but, at the same time, nudged me into keeping the store. In our negotiations, the buyer and I had hashed out several ideas for how to run things out of 1200 sq. ft. and how to do it single-handed. I built on those discussions.

The second interested buyer wanted to relocate the store 100 miles away. I was not keen on doing this since it meant a change my customers were not going to take kindly to. When she informed me the $15,000 asking price was going to be paid based on sales, and over the next 6 months with a cap of $15,000, I had some choice words for her.

As I sat there, composing that email, bashing keys and saying to myself, "She could make that money in 3 months selling just the lotions," a V8 moment hit me upside the head. I could keep the store and make the money required to have it make sense.

Against my lawyer's advice, I restructured my shop while at the same time filing a consumer proposal. This choice brought other interesting challenges, but overall it worked out better than I anticipated.

Keeping the store meant giving up my massage practice to give me time to run the store until it was making enough money to hire someone. Also, I had just laid off all my staff so it would look suspicious to hire staff again right away. It was going to be just me for a time.

Me and a lot of hard work!

I worked 14 to 17 hours a day, 7 days a week for the first 4 months to make that craziness fly but fly it did! Maybe not like a jet plane but it did take off again.

I eventually brought someone in to take over the shop while I got back to working with clients and managing the shop part-time. The other fantastic thing about pulling out of the massage practice was that I became free to transition into a coaching model. The majority of my work had always been based on energy and mindset shifting. The massage was just convenient since my clients had extended health benefits for a massage but not for coaching.

Once freed of those confines, I dove into what I most loved and was better suited for.

Through all of this, the decisiveness of a CEO, or Dominatrix, was required for me to pull off such a crazy feat. There was no way I could have undertaken that insane restructuring if I made myself wrong, second-guessed all my decisions or was not willing to lose it all.

The ability to make a choice, run with it and then course correct in the moment saved me. That, and the fact I could not go back to having a J O B. I had worked for myself for 20 years before this point. Working for a boss would have driven me mad, let alone the fact I would make a terrible employee. I am that oddball who works 80 hours a week for myself, so I don't have to work 40 hours a week for someone else.

## Inner Dominatrix Training

How do you get to the point of making fast, decisive choices?

You don't need to be in an extreme situation to learn the art of being decisive. Let's get you rolling on some tools to start the new habit.

Here are the 4 things I see as essential in being able to rock decisiveness like a Dominatrix:

1. Let go of the need to control.

2. Be willing to lose - Fuck it!

3. Let go of the judgements of yourself.

4. Get the energy read.

## Let Go of the Need to Control

It may seem ironic that the very thing that a Dominatrix is known for – control, is the very thing I am suggesting that you need to let go of. There is a difference between being 'in control,' like the master of a scene and being the 'control freak.'

Here is where the Dominatrix must do some self-checking. Control freaks are not uncommon in this world. As a Dominatrix, I met a lot of them because they got off on someone to control. Personally, I was not one for the 24/7 lifestyle of Domination. Frankly, I find it tiresome to be always 'on' and regulating someone else's life. I prefer a strong partner who is unafraid to call me on my bullshit when needed.

In life and business, the need to control leaves you tied up in knots inside because it is almost impossible to control much of anything. Not even your submissive.

The sooner you come to terms with the fact your inner control freak is not qualified to steer the ship, the smoother the waters of your life will be. It may feel like that control freak is who you need (and trust me, she screams loud to get her way) but the level-headed quiet one in the back is a better fit for your greater good.

The more you utilize the tool of expanding your energy field out - way out - the easier it is to let go. {see Appendix for more on this tool} The more you expand out, the less of a death grip you have on circumstances and the more you bob and weave around challenges. You become a Ninja Warrior of Consciousness.

Try asking yourself some questions like;

"Will this matter in 5 years?"

"If I let go of control, would I die?"

"Would anyone else die?"

These questions take the first level of serious control out of the way, allowing you to see the situation with more detachment.

The second level of question is "How can I have fun with this?"

It is hard to be serious and controlling while also having fun.

Place yourself in that state of curiosity. Avoid answering the question from your head-brain. Seek wisdom from the rest of your body instead. The head-brain loves to control and stick to what it already knows. The heart-brain puts you in touch with a sense of purpose and caring for others. Your gut-brain gives you that intuitive hit for where you need to go next.

Utilizing all these resources is like having an advisory board always available for every choice.

If you are really attached to being in control, then ask yourself "How could this turn out better if I let go of control?"

Pretend you are asking a friend the question. Then wait for the "answer." While you are waiting, go off and do something else such as take a shower, go for a walk, paint or read. Anything that pulls your mind away from answering that question lets the quieter gut and heart-brains give their input.

## Be Willing to Lose - Fuck it!

When you are willing to lose, it's easier to give up control and have fun. You will notice this loosens up the creative juices to help you find a solution you would not have seen otherwise.

The word "decisive" comes from the Latin root cedar, "to cut." Making a decision requires you to lose something to gain something. The willingness to give things up frees up your decision-making process, making it easier and more expedient.

Observing my clients and people in my workshops, I often see a pattern of needing to energetically hold on tight to what they currently have. It might be a cherished concept of who they are, possessions, or even old hurts and traumas.

This is energetic hoarding. They know this energy is not helping them. However, they are afraid of who they might be without it. Even though it is not logical or rational, the fear keeps them fully locked in.

It is rare that someone steps into the willingness to lose from merely reading about it, so do not be surprised if you don't get this concept as a result of this book. It often takes several sessions with my clients to have the idea sink in and even with that, it can take a while before they are willing to embody it.

Generally, we weed through their resistance and pry their fingers from the tight grip on all that emotional hoarding. For some, the process is strikingly similar to what we see on those reality shows about hoarders. The stress and anxiety are clearly visible when faced with clearing out things the rest of us see as garbage. I have a fascination with those shows because they physically convey what some clients face emotionally when asked to give up their energetic hoarding.

As we experience the freedom that comes from releasing old hurts, traumas, judgements and even definitions of who we are, we build this muscle of trusting the process and strengthen the willingness to lose.

I was fortunate to learn this early on in life when I chose to leave the cult I grew up in, in favour of what I knew was a better fit for me. Barely an adult, I clearly lacked the skills I needed to navigate the mostly unknown world outside of the cult. Despite that, I chose to leave everyone who cared for me. I left my community to have inner peace.

I wanted to follow what I knew to be true. I had no idea what a gift that was going to be and it took me decades to appreciate the courage it took to pack up and leave at that tender age.

My willingness to walk away from people and things as required has been a recurring theme. It gave me the freedom to speak up when I did not agree with people, systems or structures. When I saw things out of alignment with what they claimed they stood for, or when the actions they proposed were not going to bring the results they were looking for, I moved on.

Ostracized and shot down for being a troublemaker, told to fuck off, and encouraged to put up or get out, I held on to the fact that change does not come from those who toe the line or support the status quo. My willingness to lose lets me say out loud what most needs to be said.

In the end, this has been my greatest gift and my most unrelenting teacher.

I struggle with how to put into words something which is an energy you choose to step into. Typically, I demonstrate it for my clients, and they feel it while observing that modelling. Over time, they step into it more and more.

If you are not working with a good guide in this area, then do your best to stick with this process. Challenge your beliefs about what you would lose since the majority of the time our fears are entirely unfounded.

When those fears are warranted, it is good to evaluate what you would lose in comparison to what you stand to gain. Compare it to choosing between sitting on a pile of manure or sitting on a beach by the ocean. The manure may be warm and squishy at first, but it will not take long before it gets hard and stinks.

First, begin by establishing a baseline. Know where you are starting from so you can gauge if you are indeed making progress.

On a scale of 0-100, what percentage of your business are you 'willing to lose' right now? As in, walk away from it and close the doors forever. Zero being "No way in hell" and 100 being "Of course! I can walk away without a backward glance with a feeling of anticipation to see what the next chapter will bring."

This does not mean you are going to intentionally do anything to move you and your business in the direction of loss. Instead, you are willing to allow it to happen IF it was required. It is about creating more choice and more ease in your body as you move forward with growing your business.

Second, explore the idea of being willing to lose it all. Play along with me for just a moment. Jump in and see how it feels. Imagine what it would feel like to be fully surrendered to this 'willingness to lose.'

Undoubtedly, you are coming face to face with the very resistance that keeps you from being willing to drop into this energy. Fantastic!!

Third, let it surface. Take a deep breath and ask yourself if you are willing to release it. When the answer is "yes," take another deep breath and on your exhale, imagine it leaving your body.

Each day, repeat the process.

Check in to see what level you are at. Pretend you can step into the energy of being totally willing to lose it and see how that feels. As you test out this new way of being in the world, you will notice where you have resistance and blocks.

Utilize this exercise to remove it as you become aware, cleaning out new layers each time. It may seem like you are coming back again and again, but check in and see if it is a new layer. When you allow yourself to release the energy of a judgement or resistance you will feel a sense of ease or lightness in your body.

If you are not getting that feedback, then you are likely going through the motions and not releasing. This is common in the beginning. It is a muscle to develop, one that is easier to flex as you utilize and strengthen it.

Over time, the resistance to letting go dissipates, and you will discover the freedom of being willing to lose it all while playing full out to build your business. It may seem like a contradiction, but in fact, the giants in business and society are those who are willing to take huge risks and do things against the norm. Rosa Parks, Madonna, and Elon Musk are examples. They bucked the system, were called all kinds of names, even thrown in jail and carried on in spite of it all. They sparked radical changes.

We also look to the examples like Martin Luther King who led a revolution and created massive change through peaceful protest and challenging ideas. We may revere him today but take a moment to consider how much he was hated, threatened and eventually killed for his belief in a cause that was so necessary for our society. He was willing to lose it all for the sake of something bigger.

## Let go of the Judgements of Yourself!

We will dive much deeper into this subject in chapters 7 and 8, but for now know that this tool at its core, comes down to being a matter of choice. The choice is to release those self-judgements you have carried around (probably for decades) or hang on to them and continue your energetic hoarding. It is that simple. Yet so many fail to be convinced that it could be that easy.

I am challenged daily by others saying my process is a disservice to people. I'm told people need to dig down to the root causes and analyze where it is coming from and why they are hanging on to it. I'm told understanding the cause is the key to the release. While I agree wholeheartedly one must dig down deep to release the roots, I disagree with the idea it must be a slow painful process over years in a psychotherapist's office.

It takes longer for people to see they will indeed be better off without the emotional baggage then it does for them to actually release it from their system. Once a person is on-board with removing it, it becomes as easy as opening up and letting it fall away.

Imagine you are holding onto a pencil in your hand with all your might. Even though your hand cramps and you can't pick up other things due to your death grip on the pencil, you refuse to let it go. You are not sure how you even could or what it will feel like if you do or (heaven forbid) you might need that pencil and never be able to get it back. Then where would you be?

No, you decide it is best to keep holding on to that pencil just in case, regardless of how painful it is and how much it stops you from doing other things.

Once the internal gremlins (those pesky voices in your head that hate change) are firmly under control with gag balls securely in place, then letting go becomes a matter of simply opening your hand so that the pencil falls out.

The tools you choose to utilize do not matter until you realize YOU are the one that creates the shift to release the judgements. It is best to adopt a playful spirit when you use these tools. Test them out for the fun of it, not the necessity of having them work.

Energy follows intention. Ultimately, it is you creating the change. The tool itself does not matter but if it helps, then, by all means, use it. Most of us prefer a tool or a process to lean on while we learn to trust our own ability to release what is not working for us.

The Inner Dominatrix Judgement Blaster

I use this tool frequently to guide my clients into connecting with how it feels to release the judgements they hold of themselves. It might seem silly, and possibly your head-brain will tell you all the reasons why it could not possibly work.

Put all of that aside. Suspend your judgements and give it a test run.

First, allow yourself to drop in and connect to the energy of the judgement(s).

Once you connect with it, imagine grabbing it like a weed, pulling it out by the roots. Make a big messy pile of it in front of you. Pull out the judgements, pull out anything attached to them, like justifications for keeping them or insisting they are wrong/right. Dig in for any kind of righteous energy for or against the judgement.

Dig deeper and deeper until you feel a sense of ease and lightness on the topic. It is often easier to have someone guide you through it as they will nudge you deeper when there is more you could get rid of. We often delude ourselves, wanting to skim over the surface instead of moving in for even more.

Once you have taken your time to get ALL of it, now you are ready to blast it!

This is the fun part.

Throw an energy bomb at the pile of crap. Annihilate it entirely so you can not take it back.

Notice how your body feels. Lighter? More space?

Good!

Now, make a list of all the things that upset you and run each of them through this process. Clear yourself of the energetic hoarding you have become so familiar with over the years. Poke around at family issues and see what that brings up. Look at your friends, colleagues, boss, clients and neighbours. This list of people can be quite extensive. Anyone who annoys you or at least it feels that way until you blast this internal crap out of your system.

Next, look at the self-judgements you hold. Perhaps you do not love the way your body looks or maybe how you handle people (or don't handle them) bothers you.

Make a list and clear the self-judgements

A word of caution; please work with a professional for those memories that have an emotional intensity of 7/10 or higher.

This means that when you think about what happened, you gauge how much emotional intensity is stirred up. Things that are quite traumatic are best dealt with when you have someone to guide you in and out of the process.

The danger is that when you work through highly charged memories on your own, you can become overwhelmed with the emotions and no longer able to move things. In these cases, it is better to leave it alone than to poke at it and end up worse than before.

There is something I want you to really get when it comes to this Blast-it tool. Afterwards, you may be tempted to think this "thing" which you cleared has come back if you happen to feel it again a day or two down the road. Before you assume the problem lies in you, check to see if you are picking it up from someone else. Because it feels familiar, you may wrongly assume it is still yours.

We get so used to feeling disruption and dis-ease in our bodies that we can unconsciously take on someone else's energy who is also walking around with the same disruption which you recently cleared. That energy signature is so familiar you assume it is yours. Trust me on this one, it is not.

## Getting the Energy Read or Listening to the Gut-Brain

Training yourself to interpret your intuition AND following it requires time. Most of my clients take about a year or two for this to become second nature. Cut yourself some slack as you grow into this. You did not learn to walk overnight so why should this skill be instantly learned? It gets easier over time provided you are consistent in implementing it into your day-to-day life.

Let's start with some easy weights first. Select some things that don't "matter" as much to you. For instance, deciding what clothes to wear or what to order from the coffee shop. You may want to leave out the choice of who to marry or what job to say yes to until you get a little stronger in this training.

First step is always EXPAND OUT!

We are all made up of physical matter and energy. This energy is what people refer to as our Chi, or our life force, maybe even our consciousness. You have a physical body and an energetic body, the energy component is what we are going to work with and allow to expand out in all directions (360 degrees) ever expanding out (your physical body stays put) allowing the energy to go out to the size of the Universe or even out to the infinite space.

# Success Stories!

*I had a session with Dana where she first taught me about expanding out. I started expanding out every time she posted it on her Facebook page. It was a great tool to add to my tool box, but I didn't use it on a regular basis.*

*Having always loved my fast-paced niche job for the last 17 years, I was also very comfortable where I was. My life was great. It was great except for one thing. A new co-worker was giving me a hard time. I had just met a mid-range narcissist.*

*In August, I started feeling unwell, especially when 'she' (the narcissist) was around. By September, I was crying more than I was laughing and the only time I was happy was when I was away from home on race weekends and a get away with my husband. My life was falling apart and I knew things had to change.*

*In October, my doctor diagnosed me with depression. He told me to reduce the stress in my life and use the tools in my toolbox for 3 weeks and to come back and see him.*

*Daily self Reiki as well as expanding out every morning and noon became part of my routine. I started feeling better. I didn't feel as bad around my narcissist co-worker.*

*Setting an alarm to expand out on a regular basis is one of the tips Dana shared on Facebook. I tried it but didn't work for me. So I decided to pair expanding out with another frequent dally activity. I decided to expand out every time I used the ladies room. Pairing those 2 activities worked for me.*

*Expanding out allowed me to notice that the emotions that I was feeling were not mine. If they were not mine, why was I still holding on to them? So I gathered them and blasted them. It also allowed me to realize that I didn't need to stay in my hectic specialized niche and transferred to a new area, where I am happier than I was in years.*

Expanding out allows you to have perspective on your life and situations; it also allows you to feel more at ease with and in your body as you are not cramped into a small space.

As you have more space around your body you will notice that you also have more of an ability to tune into your body, you can begin to play with asking questions and see what answer feels the lightest or creates more ease in your body.

The trick is to get curious about the answer. Let go of deciding ahead of time what the outcome is going to be. This allows you to get the information from your intuition instead of that lovely brain of yours.

I know your head-brain is dying to get in there, so send it off in another direction with a different question: "Why is it so easy for me to listen to my gut-brain?"

Okay, now that we have satisfied the head-brain by giving it something to contemplate, let's play. There are various questions you can use but try these out as a starting point.

Go to your closet in the morning and pick out two shirts or two outfits and ask your body; "Body, would you like to wear this one (option A) or this one today (option B)?"

Notice which one feels lighter or more open in your body. Is it more expansive when you look at the first one or the second one? Wear the one that feels lighter for your body. That is how you lock in listening to your intuition. There is no point asking the question if you are not going to follow the answer.

Does it really matter what outfit you wear? No, it is about the training.

You are conditioning yourself to follow those gut responses - learning to lean on the wisdom of the gut-brain. In being willing to follow it in the things that do not "matter" you repeatedly condition yourself to lean on that gut-brain when it really counts - those decisions that do have a greater impact.

This tool is a way for your body to once again be your compass. Next time you are at a restaurant or coffee shop play with this tool when you are making your choice on what food or drink to order.

Relax your gaze until the whole menu is slightly blurry. Now ask your body to show you what to order. Relax and expand out more and as you do one item will become clear in your vision, and the rest will remain slightly blurry. It is as if there is a spotlight on that one item while the rest are left in the shadows and stay blurry. Now it is time to take action.

Close the menu and order that item. Do not keep looking at the menu and second-guessing yourself. I find this fun and often end up trying new things I might have otherwise missed out on.

Remember the idea is to become decisive, so choose and then move on like the Dominatrix. Allow yourself to do it wrong. Even a wrong choice can still be training for becoming decisive.

It is one meal or one drink, not a life-altering decision you are making here, so go ahead and try out the decisiveness. Put it on and see how it feels. It might feel entirely foreign at; first, that is quite alright. In fact, that is perfect because if it does not feel foreign, you are likely not changing anything.

Once you have played with these easier weights, it is time to move on to decisions that involve moving you in one direction or another. For this, you need a new set of questions for connecting to your intuition and following it.

The purpose of these questions is to ideally get you out of your brain and into the expanded awareness beyond what you are currently aware of. We all have access to the infinite knowing of the universe. However, we rarely tap into that knowledge.

So, today we are going to change that. Woo hoo!!!

Are you ready?

First, form a clear idea of your two choices: what they are and possibly what they involve (although that is not required).

Next, you are going to Expand Out! Way, way out for this! Here's how.

**Ask yourself these questions**:

> ➤ What would my life be like in five years if I do (option A)?

> ➤ What would my life be like in five years if I do (option B - or Not A if you don't have a B)?

Check the energy read on both and go with the option that feels the most expansive, or lightest. Follow it, even if that is not the logical choice.

Remember, your intuition is never wrong!

The reason we use the five-year time frame is that our head-brains have a hard time drawing conclusions on how the options would play out over that much time. Your intuitive knowing has no trouble. Also, the short-term results of an action can seem wrong, yet without making that "mistake," you would never have been in the right place at the right time for something much bigger to line up for you.

I know this sounds a bit airy-fairy, yet it has proven to be true over and over again for my clients and me. I cannot ignore the evidence that I see from personal experience.

A few years back, I debated about going to a Chamber of Commerce meeting scheduled for that evening. Now, if you have ever been to your local Chamber meetings you know, they are generally not the most fun. Too often it's a room full of stuffed shirts so stuck in their shit that it is uncomfortable for someone like me - energy sensitive and not a conformist.

Now that the day was upon me, I was turning up my nose at the idea. I had agreed to go and, having committed, I thought taking an energy read on myself would give me the out I was looking for.

I checked in using the five-year questions and got a shock at how light it felt to go to the meeting. There was no mistaking the response. It was super light to go and a bit heavy not to go. A clear winner.

I checked in a few more times during the day because I was in disbelief that a Chamber meeting was going to open up my life like that. Each time, I got the same response - super light to go.

Damn, I had to go now!

I arrived at the meeting and used an intuitive scanning technique (see Appendix A for a more in-depth explanation) to see who I needed to connect with. This makes my networking much faster and more effective.

One person who I knew as an acquaintance - Barb Stuhlemmer – 'lit up' intuitively amongst the crowd, so I headed over to talk with her. During our conversation, I asked her what she was up to lately. She told me about this "Experts Call" she ran. Once a month she brought in a guest for the show with some fun and informative nuggets for her listeners. I told her that if she needed another guest, I would be happy to be on her show and let it go.

I moved on to talk to the only other person who "lit up" for me and then I left. I spent all of 20 minutes at the Chamber Networking event.

Two weeks later Barb called me up. A guest pulled out of her Experts Call at the last minute and could I fill in? I made it work despite some interesting logistical challenges for the call on my end.

Because of that call, I hired Barb to map out a strategy for my coaching work and how to bring the Dominatrix spin into the world. During our strategy session, she suggested I connect with Cindy Ashton and become a sponsor for her upcoming event. Cindy turned into a client and is now a raving fan. She, in turn, connected me to numerous clients and put me on her TV Show - Cindy Uncorked - as one of her regular experts.

All this from being willing to follow my inner knowing and ignore my brain screaming at me not to go the Chamber meeting. I clearly knew nothing compared to what my intuition knew.

This kind of thing happens regularly when you follow your inner knowing instead of your head-brain.

# Chapter 4

# HOW TO RECEIVE

Sitting on one of the best chairs in the house I found myself with a sweet submissive man who said nothing but simply slid himself in at my feet and looked up at me with that anticipation of "Will I be accepted?"

He quietly asked if he could serve me tonight.

I told him I was drinking whiskey, straight, no ice and let him know which bottle was mine as this was a private, invitation-only house party and BYOB.

He leaped up with a palpable air of excitement, obviously elated to be of service.

It was by no means a complicated drink, but still, the speed with which he returned was remarkable. I nodded my appreciation, taking care not to make too much fuss over him. He was a slave after all, and it is customary to be sparing in doling out praise to your submissive.

Once my drink was securely delivered, he slid himself back into the small space at my feet and asked if he could have permission to massage my feet. When I said yes, I thought he would burst from joy. He put real love and care into massaging and caressing my feet for hours, grateful for any task that allowed him to serve.

Sitting at my feet, a thing that most people see as degrading and demeaning, he found utter joy.

Meanwhile, I was in turmoil. This was early days for me on the Dominatrix side of the coin, and I felt shocked at how hard it was to sit there and receive.

I grew up with the belief that women served their men, so this turn of roles was utterly foreign to me. I enjoyed it for sure but, at the same time, it challenged all the programming of my upbringing. The internal rush and excitement locked horns with the "Who are you to be receiving? This isn't your role!"

I sat there, suppressing the overwhelming urge to yank my boots back on and run out of the party as fast as I could.

Intellectually, I knew this was all part of the deal but putting it into practice was a whole different ball of wax. I had no idea how to allow people to serve me.

As fate would have it, there was another Mistress in the room being lovingly served by her slave. A Mistress who willingly shared her insights about being a Domme. She shared the joy of holding loving power and fulfilling a submissive's desire to serve and please her. Knowing the exchange is mutually beneficial, she could relax into taking charge.

As she spoke, I tapped into her energy (similar to modelling behaviour but with energy instead) and allowed myself to try it on as my own submissive sat at my feet. I sat taller in the chair, imagining the presence of a Queen who serves her people by standing as a ruler and allowing them to serve so she may hold court with grace.

The ruling Queen must allow others to attend to details such as cooking and cleaning, ushering in guests and much more, so she can sit on the throne and command respect. The people look to her to rule, and she only rules when she allows others to serve her.

So, too, as a Dominatrix, I could not hold this power if I was running around. The more I allowed myself to receive, the more he enjoyed his service. It was not about me having power over him. It was about being strong and of service by holding the power for him to fill his role.

It is in the "not doing," in requiring the submissive to serve that the Dominatrix is free to fill the role of power and control.

As I grew into my role as a Dominatrix, I came to see how important it was for me to receive fully and to stand in that power so others could surrender and completely let go. It was good for both of us when I allowed that beautiful exchange to unfold.

In general, we suck at receiving. Give someone a compliment and 9 times out of 10, women will cringe and deflect it. If you tell them they look great in an outfit, they often move to "This old thing? Ugh. I have had this for years."

They skip right over receiving the compliment and move into downplaying it. Or they redirect and turn it back to you very quickly in an attempt to return the favour.

It seems most women (and even some men) never learned to soak up a compliment and treat it as a gift. Growing up, we witnessed our mothers, grandmothers and aunts doing this dance and we emulated the same behaviour.

But here's the thing -- rushing past or downplaying a compliment is rude to the giver. You are trampling on the gift just presented to you.

It's like smashing it in front of them and tossing it in the garbage.

This may sound harsh, but energetically that is what you are doing and what many have been conditioned to do. While the analogy is jarring, it is also effective to encourage people to give up this behaviour.

Not accepting a compliment hinders them from moving forward in other ways because it is not just about being able to receive compliments. That is only one symptom of our inability to receive.

As a coach, I say all kinds of crazy things to jolt people out of where they are stuck. I do this to give them the ability to launch into something new. It is the verbal cracking of the whip to put things in perspective.

I love watching people's reactions when I fully receive their compliments. They, in turn, receive from me at the same time. Just like giving someone a gift they gush over when our compliment is fully embraced we feel warmth and love return to us. Trust me. You are doing them a favour by allowing yourself to take it in.

Receiving only becomes comfortable when you practice it over and over again. Disregard your social conditioning. Ignore the chatter of your head-brain attempting to coerce you into playing small and modest, as if being modest gets you closer to what you are aching to create.

Modesty and humility are lovely attributes in moderation. So are hot peppers but when you over do it, it upsets the digestive system. In the same way, overuse of modesty and humility becomes tiresome and unattractive.

So how does receiving a compliment relate to other areas of your life and business?

The "muscle" you use to receive a compliment is the very same "muscle" you need to flex to receive money.

How do you respond to people when they compliment you? How often do you say yes to offers of help? If you are having trouble bringing in money consistently, then examine how well you receive in general.

Begin by learning to receive a compliment and then move into other types of receiving. Because you encounter compliments in your daily life, this gives you the chance to practice regularly the art of truly receiving without fluffing over or deflecting. Soak it in like a decedent bath.

Receiving help in business is another trap for the entrepreneur. It is tempting to want to prove yourself, so you adopt the mindset of needing to do it all yourself. Maybe you are so focused on how hard it is that you don't even recognize when people hold out an offer to help,

Take a moment and reflect. How are you at receiving help in your business?

Do you say yes when someone steps forward to assist with a task or fill a gap in your skills? If not, you miss the beautiful exchange of allowing others to help you which in turn robs them of the joy of giving.

A tip that may serve you to receive is the following:

Stepping into the energy of the Inner Dominatrix, you open yourself up to others to assist you. You gift people the joy of a service rendered by allowing yourself to receive. They feel seen and appreciated, completing the circle of giving and receiving. Perhaps the receiving comes in the form of valuable connections, or maybe it is constructive criticism on your work. By surrendering to receiving help, your business grows faster.

The Dominatrix can show you a different way of being in and with your business that makes it more enjoyable for everyone -- if you allow it!

**Action**

Reach out to someone who offered to help you recently, and let them provide their knowledge or skills. No matter how uncomfortable you find this at first, the more you learn to receive and surrender into it the easier it becomes.

The skill of receiving deepens each time you apply it. Being masterful at receiving takes some time. It is okay if it is bumpy and awkward at first.

Take action and blast away the resistance and judgements that come up. There is a good chance they are not even yours anyway.

# The Orgasm of Receiving

Inspiration hit during a session with a client who felt challenged in bringing in the kind of money she required for her business to be solvent and make it worth her time.

An amazingly talented woman, she worked hard to get things going. She hired a business coach and paid out some serious coin for that coaching. The unfortunate thing was she really needed to work with me first because she couldn't pull the trigger and take action on all the great business coaching she received.

Susan is an artistic, creative, and uber-talented wordsmith who is also well connected to her sexual (in the bedroom) energy and able to let go and enjoy some incredible sexual experiences.

But...

She was also a control freak and fought me by trying to analyze all the individual processes logically before she would let things go. It severely hindered the speed in which the limitations and beliefs were released. Running through it mentally is painfully slow as each limitation must be thoroughly evaluated before it is let go.

Susan had indicated that time was of the essence and we needed to get her pulling in more money FAST. Her control side felt like dragging an anchor on our work together, so I looked for an analogy that would allow her to surrender. I needed one she could connect to and not resist.

In that moment, brilliance (aka drawing on the collective intelligence) kicked in and brought with it this sexy analogy.

When you are just about to orgasm, your body requires you to relinquish control and allow it to wash over you like a wave of pure joy, even possibly mixed with pain. Without surrender, the orgasm may be missed or shortened. You cannot force it, push it along or control it. Your job is to surrender into it, enjoy. Relax and go with the flow.

Now imagine that the Universe is your lover. A very experienced lover who has studied the art of love making for millennia. This is a lover who derives his pleasure from bringing you to the ultimate orgasm.

Would you be trying to control this highly skilled lover attending to you with passion, desire and working his well-honed skills?

No, my dear, you would relax and enjoy!

Well, this is what receiving money is about. Money is the orgasm, and the Universe is your expert lover, ready to bring you to multiple orgasms over and over and over. Allow yourself to surrender to the expertise of your lover.

For my client, this was the exact analogy required for her to loosen the control grip dramatically. She visibly relaxed and drank in the bliss of this concept.

The other analogy I often use with clients to nudge this release of the control freak is to imagine being at a restaurant.

You arrive with three of your dear friends. You sit down, order some drinks and after you decide what you will eat, you place your order with the server.

Do you then get up every five minutes to ask the server if your order is ready?

Do you call your server over and re-order your dinner every five minutes?

Do you get up and go into the kitchen and try to help the cook with your meal?

No! That would be ridiculous.

Instead, you enjoy your wine and the company of your friends and relax, knowing that at some point your food will arrive and you will eat.

Unfortunately, some people place orders with the Universe and then try to control when or how the order will arrive. Or they change their order, which delays the delivery because things have to start all over in the kitchen to create your new request.

Let go and trust the Cook (the Universe) to bring what you asked for.

For some people who insist the Control Freak must remain firmly intact and in charge, I remind them that customers who are a pain in the ass end up with food that is spat in.

I once watched a documentary about the restaurant industry, and this is a real thing. Servers would spit in the food of the customers who were a royal pain in the ass. A server can't tell the customers off so unfortunately, this passive aggressive behaviour comes out.

No one enjoys being micromanaged.

Think of it this way. What if your constant need to meddle is costing you in the quality of what and how much you receive?

Something interesting happens when a person intellectually analyzes their emotions and memories, dissecting them into their finest points, all in a drive to "understand" or "make sense" of them.

In my early days of therapy, I spent hours in analysis pulling apart what happened, why it happened and how that led to my reactive behaviour. It fascinated me, and my logical brain had a field day with this process.

The problem is, in the end, it was all crap I no longer needed. Those old behaviours failed to serve me, and the emotional baggage acted like a boat anchor in my life.

While analysis is intriguing, the more efficient path utilizes energy psychology tools to disconnect the emotional charge from the memories and re-write the programs. These tools can be as simple as taking a deep breath and visualizing releasing the emotion and energy attached to a memory. Or being guided to connect with your sub-programs to replace them with programming that serves you more effectively.

For example, imagine pulling out the programs in your body telling you it is not safe to earn more than "enough" money. Clearing away the judgements and attachments rewrites the programs and allows you to enjoy as much wealth as you choose.

Once those programs and energy shift then you can look back from a place of detachment. In a few moments, you grasp the full depth of what happened, why it happened and what your gifts were from it.

Given the magnitude of baggage, most people carry it is good news to know tools exist to speed up the process

If you are one of those caught up in "analysis paralysis," think about it this way: all that emotional baggage, all the hurts, anger, resentment, fear, disillusionment and so on, they are basically the poop in your toilet.

You could choose to put on a pair of gloves and get in there. You could sort through your shit, discovering what was digested and what was not, noticing the nuggets of undigested corn or other items. Would you pull out that kernel of corn and set it aside for reuse later?

Yuck! I do hope you are gagging from the thought of reaching into that toilet. It is crap! Crap you are ready to be done with. It only requires a flush to remove it from your premises.

But this is precisely what you do on an emotional and energetic level by rehashing and overanalyzing the shit you went through.

What if you chose to flush it energetically, recognizing it as poop without the need to feel it, smell it or even taste it to make sure it truly is shit? Instead, hit that cosmic flush lever and be done with it.

I have been challenged on this idea many times by "experts" who say real healing only happens when you understand what happened and you "do the core work." As someone who has spent long hours over decades in a wide variety of psychologist, psychotherapist, and energy psychotherapist offices, I can assure you the end result is the same. However, the cost and the time to get to a place of understanding, acceptance and (eventually) gratitude was light years faster with energy-based psychotherapy.

Do what works for you. Maybe that is traditional therapy, and perhaps that is energy healing or yoga. We all must pick the path most aligned for us as individuals.

If you are a busy business owner, you may not have the luxury of years of therapy to understand one slice of your childhood. You need a grasp on your emotions now to find some peace and gratitude so you can take your business to new heights while also expanding as a human being. In a world reaching epic proportions of chaos, you need to quickly find your equanimity.

Being a leader in your business, your home or just with yourself is mainly dependent on your ability to move past or around the obstacles with the least amount of emotional upheaval. Your inner clearing of the crap and baggage IS vital to your business success, not to mention your mental health.

# Chapter 5

# WHAT FUCKING COMFORT ZONE?

## Breaking the so-called comfort zone

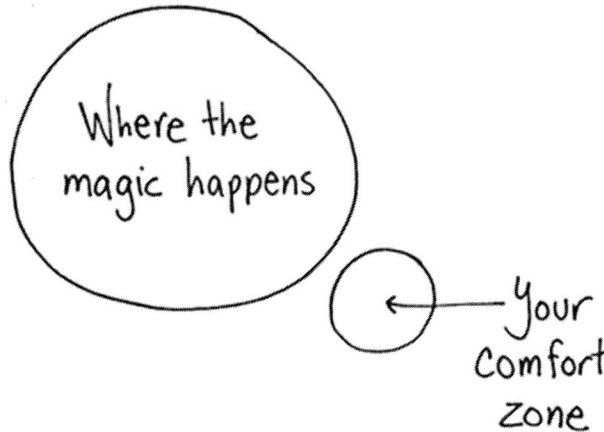

"You need to get out of your comfort zone."

How many times have you heard this spouted as if it were Gospel?

How many "thought" leaders and facilitators have you heard repeat this in their talks or workshops? And don't get me started with how many times a day this gets posted all over social media?

For years, business and mindset gurus have touted this "growth happens outside your comfort zone" as if it were

THE life-saving mantra. While the concept is one I agree with in theory, there is an inherent flaw in following this as a model to live by or to motivate yourself to step into the unknown.

I would even go so far as to say it is dangerous.

It sounds very sexy, and in theory, it would seem accurate. People are not changing because they are too comfortable with where they are currently.

However, I have two issues with this saying.

The first issue is that, when it comes to changing what is not working, there is an underlying assumption you are comfortable with the way things are in your so-called "comfort zone." From what I have seen in myself and my clients over the past 25 years I strongly disagree. If you were comfortable with those things, then you would not identify them as needing to change, right? If that's true, then how can it be your comfort zone?

If we take a look at being overweight as an example, are you actually comfortable carrying around that extra weight? If you tell me you are looking to slim down, then you cannot be at ease with your weight. If you were comfortable with this weight, then you would not be looking to change it.

I believe what most gurus refer to as 'the comfort zone' is actually a form of cognitive dissonance.

Cognitive dissonance happens when our actions are out of line with our beliefs and values. We craft stories and justifications to validate our actions in an attempt to reconcile the disconnect between our values and beliefs. It seems more natural to re-write the internal dialogue rather than change the behaviours.

We gravitate to compromises and excuses instead of making adjustments to our actions. This is not something we consciously decide; instead, it is a subconscious behaviour when people are unwilling, to be honest with themselves. It explains why they choose to behave as they do.

So, in our example of the weight, on the inside, we are not happy with where we are physically (not to mention all the social pressures). Yet we are unwilling to do what it takes to change the weight. Instead, we change the story we tell ourselves and others. We find reasons to make it not that bad or even acceptable to stay the weight we are.

When we re-write the supporting story, we create cognitive dissonance.

Let's say we tell people we are content with a few extra pounds on or that we would "rather be happy than thin" or "I love food and refuse to deny myself." Maybe we claim it is our thyroid and no matter how much we cut back we can't lose the weight so why bother?

We know these are half-truths at best and downright lies at times. We tell them to avoid looking squarely in the mirror and admitting to ourselves what we are actually up to.

We tell ourselves lies, so we feel better about not changing the behaviour. We often do this because changing the core programming feels threatening to our existence, so we hang on to what feels 'safer.

These new stories are the so-called comfort zone. The problem is that no matter how well crafted your story may be, your subconscious knows the truth.

Each time you tell yourself these creative stories, you hear that quiet nagging voice that whispers, "Lies... all lies..."

You create in your body a low-grade dis-ease.

Over time this disconnect will find a way to capture your attention. All the mind-body research over the years proves that our emotions do in fact affect our physical health. When we choose to lie to ourselves repeatedly, we set up the body for dysfunction as it struggles to cope with the misalignment between our values and our behaviours.

Bring yourself back into alignment with your true core values, which you may need to rediscover and reconnect with first. Taking steps to ensure your actions reflect those core values will ultimately bring you peace and healing. That is the harmony your body so desperately seeks to re-connect with.

So, when people tell me they need to get out of their comfort zone, it confuses me.

What I see is a person who is not comfortable, I ask myself, "Where is the fucking comfort zone?"

What if there was no such thing?

What if, in order to change, you were merely exchanging one discomfort for a different discomfort?

I fail to see any evidence that the comfort zone theory is helping people to move out of where they are stuck to where they can create change. I am not convinced the presentation of this concept has caused anyone to move out of the so-called comfort zone, to choose change.

Does it move you? Or does it give you a reason to hold back from changing?

"Oooh, I don't want to give up my comfort zone."

Or "That is why it is hard to change; it's my comfort zone" thus locking in the belief that change is hard.

It can feel dangerous and almost life threatening to re-write these stories that were created to keep you safe, to keep you in a space that feels familiar. The reality is this familiar zone is not where you experience joy and ease with your body. It is merely known to you, and those parts of you responsible for keeping you safe would rather stick with something crappy rather than risk stepping out into the unknown. When you attempt to move into the unfamiliar territory, your 'unsafe' alarms trigger a warning. The only way they know to keep you 'safe' is to keep you out of anything that has not been tested or explored.

So your days become more of the same old, same old, day in and day out.

If you have ever felt like you have been looping around the same issues over and over, this may be your clue. You are not risking new territory to get a new result.

These 'unsafe' alarms for most people have become highly sensitive, going off when they are not needed or wanted. It is like a car alarm that goes off with the wind blowing on it. Our internal signals are going off far too often and without being evaluated or recalibrated.

What if you were to look at your situation from the perspective of "no comfort zone"? Would this compel you to move into action, seeking to bring about harmony in your body? Dialling down the hyper-sensitive 'unsafe' alarms in your system?

The second issue I have with this concept is the unspoken idea that the discomfort you are in is far more comfortable than the discomfort of change.

---

If you are not comfortable where you are, and you are taught that changing is going to feel worse, is it any wonder we are a society of people unwilling to change?

Take a moment to consider this. When it comes to something you identified as needing to change -- have you ever been comfortable with it? Have you ever loved that extra 20 lbs and thought "Ah, this extra fat is so comfortable"? Have you ever been comfortable with not having enough money to pay the bills?

Let's get real with this!

It is not bloody well comfortable nor is it likely to become comfortable. Think of it more like wetting the bed. For a brief moment, it is warm and feels good. That moment is very short as things cool quickly, the smell hits your nostrils, and you feel a world of shame.

You may lay there for a while, not wanting to face the embarrassment when the rest of your family finds out. But eventually it gets so gross, you're forced out of bed to do something about the situation.

I see this as a more fitting analogy than the so-called "comfort zone." From my experience personally and working with clients, the discomfort becomes so strong it overrides any made-up resistance and fears your mind has cleverly created.

When we turn to science for a moment, we discover the research is on our side in this matter. The way the body responds to fear is so close to how it responds to the excitement that we could call these responses identical twins.

Note that I am referring to anxiety-type fear, not the life-threatening fear of being chased by a tiger or having someone put a gun to your head. That is a different kind of fear, and while similar, it is not the same as excitement. Fortunately, life-threatening situations are not a regular occurrence for most of us on this planet. If you are reading this book, then you likely live in an environment mostly free from this kind of fear.

Most of us, however, treat anxiety-fear as if it were life-threatening. It sends our bodies into full-out flight or fight response, firing off the adrenaline and tensing up, ready for action. However, the action never comes, and we never utilize that adrenaline for our fast sprint to outrun the tiger. Instead, our body must get rid of the adrenaline and calm the nervous system.

Repeated triggers of this adrenal response put you in line for burnout and health complications. Your adrenal gland eventually waves the white flag, desperately hoping it can surrender and give up this repeating loop.

Anxiety-fear and excitement, like those identical twins, seem impossible to tell apart. Yet when you know them well, you notice subtle differences and can see them individually. A stranger may have a hard time telling the difference between identical twins, but their mother recognizes them. She knows her twins intimately and sees the almost imperceptible differences between them.

If you get to know fear and excitement so intimately that you can tell them apart, then you will understand where you have been slapping the fear label on things that should be labelled excitement.

What if this so-called "stepping outside the comfort zone" was actually exciting to you? The fact your heart beats a little stronger, and your breath quickens could, in fact, be evidence of the excitement.

We get conditioned from an early age to identify fear. We require this skill for our survival. This conditioning becomes a problem because we rarely get taught how to differentiate fear from excitement. We end up labelling everything as fear since they feel so much alike.

So, if you aren't comfortable with where you are, why not trade it for a different discomfort -- one that moves you in the direction you want to go instead?

To me, that seems like a more plausible and motivating mantra that engages people and shifts them into action. Given that there is NO comfort zone, do you really want to be stuck in the crap you are sitting in, feeling uncomfortable in that piss-soaked bed?

Or will you choose to get up and change the sheets?

Roll it around for a bit. I just challenged your tried and true mantra so it might take a while to sink in fully. If you are willing to connect with this radical idea that allows you to choose change, I'll wait.

In the meantime, let's take things in a different direction; let's look at this from a universal consciousness perspective.

If we step into the woo-woo world idea that "everything is connected" and "time is not real," then what if this whole comfort zone concept is a game we play in order to dance with the experience of struggle? And what if the struggle is just one of the many experiences we are gifted with because we live in a physical body?

I love the idea that we are all Infinite Beings having human experiences. This concept entirely resonates in my body and my soul. At its core, it creates an ease with being in my body and life exactly as it is, right here and right now.

Slipping into a place where nothing "needs" to change, it becomes a matter of choice to change or not.

Sit with that for a moment. What if nothing NEEDED to be changed? How does that feel in your body?

Giving up the necessity of things and moving through life with a playful attitude helps you find the joy in change, the fun in discomfort. You change merely because you can.

I recognize this may not be a perspective that works for everyone. Stepping into Dominatrix Energy means first doing what works for you and not compromising your values and beliefs for anyone else. As with all the concepts in this book, take what you love and leave the rest.

Just be sure you are not choosing the familiar over the discomfort of the unknown. Trust your intuitive knowing to guide you as your head-brain defaults to what is known and familiar to keep you "safe." However, "safe" is not where the magic happens. After all, "safe" is really an illusion. If you are an Infinite Being, what is there to actually need to be safe from?

The Dominatrix invites you to surrender into the discomfort of the unknown rather than fighting to remain in the discomfort of the familiar. This principle can be applied to anything in your life. Slowly ramping up the level of uncomfortable (aka unfamiliar) activities allows you to surrender. When you release the need to fight change, things become more comfortable.

It also helps to add a dash of 'fuck it' and do the action despite your resistance.

Remember, the submissive surrenders into the pain of a whip or a spanking by breathing deeply and allowing their body to relax into that magical journey. The slow ramping up of intensity enables the body to release the endorphins which in turn will allow them to tolerate more of the pain and experience more of the rush.

As the Dominatrix, your surrender into the flow will call for you to get there without the aid of someone to push you, without someone to make sure that you keep going. You are the one in charge of the pace and making sure that the scene continues. This means that you are going to need to dig deeper and find your 'why,' your internal reason for moving past any anxiety-fear that may pop up as you move forward.

This is why many choose to hire coaches or join mastermind groups. These outside support systems keep you accountable and on track with your desired outcomes on those days when you can't seem to make yourself do it, or when your 'unsafe' alarms may be going off needlessly. These people allow you to lean into the 'pain' of change, reminding you of the bigger picture and who you are at the core – an Infinite Being!

When you learn to surrender, releasing the struggle and fight, ever expanding out to be more, you receive more and live more.

**Putting this into Action**

Make a list of things you believe you are afraid of.

In fact, I created space for you to make that list right here and right now. No time quite like the present.

Commit to doing them. Just not all at once because that is asking for disaster. Pick one and keep doing that activity until it becomes comfortable or at least, less of a challenge.

For example, if speaking to strangers is hard for you now then commit to talking to one stranger every day until it is no longer raises your blood pressure.

You will, of course, want to utilize the tool of "blasting out" (see Appendix for more) the resistance and internal self-judgements that creep up as engage in your new activity. Breathe. Lean into the pain. Breathe it in like a sweet, succulent jasmine fragrance filling the night skies.

If you are the type that loves to go for the brownie points and play full out, then I challenge you to take your morning shower with cold water every morning for two weeks and prep yourself to do the hard things.

Yes, I do mean starting with the water full cold.

And yes, I do mean every day for two full weeks.

If you lived somewhere that had nothing but cold water for the next two weeks, you would muster up the courage to jump in and get scrubbed off before getting on with your day. It's not that you can't physically do this challenge. Instead, you think it will be harder than it's actually going to be.

I love giving this assignment to my private clients. Beyond the incredible mental and physical benefits of the task, it is a fantastic way to turn up the volume on the mental chatter and resistance we employ to "prove" we are not capable of changing an aspect of our lives - such as our weight or our money. As you stand before a shower pouring out cold water, your brain spews out every reason and justification in the world to keep you from stepping in and shocking your body.

After a few days of this you will find it is not nearly as bad as your head-brain thought and after the full two weeks, you've proven to yourself you can do the hard thing.

You realize you are capable of far more than you gave yourself credit for.

After those two weeks, your hot shower feels like a decadent treat, and quite likely, it won't be as hot as it was before this challenge.

# Success Stories!

*On October 5th, my life changed dramatically. My husband of 8 years woke up to stroke-like symptoms and within 5 days, nothing was getting better. After seeing the MRI results, there was no brain activity left, and I had to decide to take him off life support. My husband Derek died peacefully with me along side. The grieving process had now begun.*

*Over the next 6 months, Dana helped me get back on track with my life. Having to go through the path of grief and also Post Traumatic Stress Disorder, she allowed me the space and time to work through the emotions I needed in order to heal. One of the things I learned from Dana is how important it is to create a space for people without trying to fix their pain.*

*With a life experience so drastic, I am humbled to know that Dana stepped up to the plate to help me work through, expand out, and allow myself to be in those darkest of moments. This is highly important when moving through the concepts of grief, is to allow yourself to feel these emotions. As an individual, I always tried to see the light in everything, ignoring whatever kind of darkness there is, however Dana provided me with an understanding that there is light and dark in everything.*

*This understanding allowed me to own my grief, to be okay with what I am going through, and acknowledge that grief is a process to walk through. The symptoms pertaining to grief are drastic, long, and with PTSD, the healing process was not going to happen overnight. Her tools helped me continue to the process of healing for my future. There is energy all around and to know that we don't have to sit in the muck of grief, we can drop down to our heart centre, acknowledge it, and continue to walk through it because "this too shall pass." Within the first year and a bit after losing Derek, I was able to begin my steps in moving forward, applying for my Masters of Education, find a new partner, enjoy and love life again along my own path.*

~ Jen CB (Jennifer Casement Buttineau)

# Chapter 6

# WORK LIKE THE MONEY DOESN'T MATTER

## Money is Not Real

From the moment you step into the Dungeon, your focus needs to shift, so you become fully engaged with what is going on. You must mentally leave everything else outside the door: your kids, the dishes, the list of tasks yet to be accomplished. Distractions that have not paid to be here will keep you from performing at your peak. They are unwelcome voyeurs in the Dungeon.

For most jobs, you can show up and be distracted, work half-assed and still collect your pay. Not in the Dungeon!

Your client expects and requires that you BRING IT every time, no matter what happened to you five minutes or five days before that moment. They need you to pay attention. The stakes are quite high. In fact, they have put their life and their emotional well-being in your hands, so it is time for you to step it up. Get fully present and stay that way for the whole session.

If it sounds like I am being dramatic, think again. This degree of focus is required to play at this level, and it is the same focus you need to play a bigger game in your business. Your game face needs to be on and stay on.

The other big distraction that pulls many hobby Mistresses off their game is a focus on the money. Thinking of the client in terms of how much money a session is worth, how much you can talk them into or how much they may tip are all examples of being focused on the money.

That kind of distraction is a career killer. When you are here just for the money, your drive and motivation shift. Eventually, you will lose your taste for what you are doing. At this point, many pro-Dommes slide into drugs or alcohol to keep the game going, which is dangerous for everyone involved.

Beyond the obvious issue of safety for all players when one is high, stoned or drunk, there is also an erosion of the soul. To work only for the money in a field often disrespected (certainly not one you would brag about at a country club event) leaves you feeling depleted and empty on the inside. That leads to more drugs and alcohol to mask your pain.

It is not unlike the stereotypical strippers who are there for the money and have not come to terms with the work. Slowly, life bleeds out. They need a libation to make the shift pass so they can make their quota to buy their drug of choice. The cycle repeats over and over.

The money can be good, but you are going to work your ass off for it. Beating people is a very physically demanding job. There are also mental and emotional strains with each session. You are required to be fully on with 100% of your energy and emotion. You need to be on high alert for their non-verbal signs as well as physically able to dish out punishment for a sustained period of time.

This is the reason I now call myself the Lazy Dominatrix. I prefer energy and mindset tools for the same overall outcome for my client (minus the delicious reminder bruises, of course). I still bring them to the space of surrender, but in a way, they can re-create on their own.

I see the same money distraction in business. Being focused on how much each client means in dollars pulls you away from serving deeply. It is easy to become dissatisfied with the small annoying challenges until the money itself is not enough.

As an antidote, I challenge my clients to play different roles in their business.

Let's say you run a marketing company. When you interact with your clients, interview them about their needs or craft their marketing materials, you wear those particular hats and money has nothing to do with those positions. Since the business manager and accountant do not interact with clients, you would not wear those hats to engage with a client. You focus on serving deeply, connecting with them and having them surrender to your expertise.

However, when you need to do up their invoice, you put on your accounting or business manager hat and manage the money. The business manager is also in charge of making sure the systems run smoothly, and you (as the service provider) hit your targets.

I am not suggesting your focus on serving the client gives you permission to give services away for free. I am certainly not recommending that.

What I am pointing out is a way to disconnect from the significance and attachment most of us have placed on money. Adding the weight of "If I have money it means this" or "If I don't have money it means this" to customer service is never helpful.

We could fill several books with the enormous amounts of shit people have about money. Much of it is not even theirs, but for the sake of staying on track, I am going to stay high-level with this for you. Undoubtedly you have read several books about money before picking up this one so refer back to some of the better ones.

The actual amount of money in our possession does not determine our emotional or energetic baggage about money. I have seen millionaires burdened with limiting programs around money. I have worked with people who have very little money and yet they have a tremendous amount of ease with it, trusting that more will show up and it always does. The physical having of money is not the cause of the baggage (or lack of baggage).

Far too often, people get attached to the belief that their lack of money creates the scarcity mindset which they are married to. Yet that theory flies out the window with my own personal experience and from what I have seen with clients. This is what led to my "money is not real" concept.

Do we all need money? Yes

Can we change or eliminate our "limiting beliefs" about money?

Yes, if you choose. These beliefs are basically set up in our subconscious brains as programs and programs can be re-written.

There are thousands of books, seminars and programs specifically targeted at helping you to drop the baggage and old beliefs about money. Some are helpful to some degree, but most are a waste of time because unfortunately, they keep you locked in but still feeling like things are changing. This is so they can sell you the next program while dangling a few people who have supposedly succeeded with their method.

Full disclosure: I am sick of seeing people getting sucked in by these false gurus. It's why I am so passionate about people standing in their Inner Dominatrix energy so they can be their own guru instead of looking outside for it.

Money – and the beliefs one has about money and what it says about you -- is one of the biggest pitfalls for people. It causes them to slide into making themselves wrong. It is so easy to compare yourself to what you think others have based on what you see, or to focus on what you think you do not have and therefore makes you wrong.

In fact, look at all the marketing out there. The top selling products are about how to make big money or easy money. Coming in a close second are the millions of diet programs and weight loss solutions. Tugging on your belief that there is something wrong with you, they twist that knife to make it even more painful and then offer a magic solution to ease your pain.

The money issue or weight issue or family issue are all symptoms of the same underlying core dynamic. The real problem is you buy into the idea there is something wrong with you. That puts you on the lookout for evidence of how you are fucked up. In your search for how you are wrong, you fail to see how amazing, brilliant and powerful you actually are.

The idea that "what you focus on grows" is likely not a new concept to you. When we apply it to money your "money issue" become your focus. Are you staring squarely at the lack of money coming in? If so, that is precisely what is going to show-up - a lack of money.

Now, let's go a bit deeper. What creates that focus on lack? What are you telling yourself about your ability to generate more money? Is it that you are brilliant? Not likely. I would bet big dollars you are highly judgemental of what you are doing, how you are doing it and why you get the results you do.

By addressing and changing the internal self-judgement programs running in your system, the root of the money problem is also addressed.

As I take clients on this core journey, it is inspiring to see things fall into place even when we were not focused on that. Incomes go up. Weight slips away. Family conflicts ease. All as a result of doing this core work around owning their brilliance and power.

To keep moving forward remind yourself on a regular basis what your motivation is. Your "Why."

What is it that pulls you out of bed? What has you excited to jump into another round of sales calls or promoting your business?

I have not met many people who can keep going with a business just for the money. Some can at first because let's face it, we need to have our basics covered. A roof over our heads and food on the table. However, once those basics are taken care of, we move up the pyramid of Maslow's Hierarchy of Needs and find we now require a stronger sense of purpose to keep going. Especially those who identify with the "heart-centred entrepreneur" label.

Money in and of itself lacks the warm fuzzy you need to keep going when people judge you or when bill collectors call while you are waiting for customers to pay. Faced with challenges, it is easy to get pulled into the money trap. This is the thinking that only sees what is missing and the stuff not done. That path leads to feeling like a pile of crap and pulling the covers over your head instead of getting out there.

What if you opted to view money as not real? What if you could shatter the illusion you have clung to up until now about money? About having it or not having it?

This may seem simplistic, but the more I dig into the concept of money beliefs, the more I witness how our beliefs about money and the story we tell about ourselves are what creates the results in our bank account. The more we are attached to the idea of money being hard and a struggle to get, the heavier it feels to create.

That weight of the emotional attachment then spills over into our activities. When we talk with potential clients, and we are entrenched in fear, they feel that underlying fear when you "pitch" them or talk about fees. That scarcity energy is, of course, repelling to clients and they will not be drawn to work with you.

When you let yourself drop into that delicious space of KNOWING the money is coming, even when you don't have proof, then things start lining up for you in ways that are not logical and not linear. This is the "not real" of money to which I am referring to.

Choosing to see money as "not real" allows you to open up to those inspired ideas and take action, which brings in what you are asking for.

The more you use tools to clear out the energetic attachments to your current beliefs about money, having it or not having it and all the wonderfully creative stories you have concocted about money, the easier it becomes to open up to choosing to see money as "not real."

After you have managed to shake loose the idea that money is real and therefore powerful or something out of your control, then I invite you to consider rejecting the concept of limiting beliefs in the first place. Step out of that mess with grace instead and stop seeing yourself as broken and in need of 'fixing.'

You can still use the tools to clear out these beliefs, but from the perspective of play and "just because" rather than needing to do it because you are broken. The action looks exactly the same on the outside. However, on the inside you are shifting things faster because YOU are the one in charge; YOU get to say what stays and what goes.

The more you own your Inner Dominatrix, the less you make yourself wrong and the more you go for what you desire to create in this world.

Please note this is a process, but one worth every ounce of effort you put into sticking with it.

# Chapter 7

# JUDGEMENT IS A WASTE
# OF YOUR ENERGY

## How to tell a Judgement from Awareness

I love how much discussion gets created when I raise the topic of how to determine if something is a judgement vs. an awareness/discernment. There is no end to the debate on this topic nor should there be. Discussion leads to deeper understanding and awareness when approached with an open mind.

Let's start with how I define the word "judgement."

When I invite a discussion on social media by asking, "Could you ever be free of judgement?" I quickly come to see many people define the word in a way synonymous with discernment or maybe cognitive processing. As a result, they see judgement as vital to everyday life and making decisions which I completely agree with. When you are driving your car, you need to assess how fast the other vehicles are going or what they are likely to do to keep from crashing into them. That is a beneficial skill.

When I refer to judgement in this book, however, I am talking about the concept of assigning something a right or wrong label and then attaching an emotion and a meaning to that label.

For example, if we see ourselves as wrong and therefore bad and/or ashamed, then we are up to our eyeballs in judgements of ourselves. That energy locks up our systems to some degree. When you become attached to the meaning and the need to make something wrong in your mind, it locks the judgement in place.

When I refer to awareness in this book, I am talking about connecting with your inner guidance system, a place of knowing without processing. Some would call it intuitive knowing, or gut-brain. There are many names for the same brilliance residing within you, which is a resource too often left untapped.

Discernment is more of a cognitive process, sifting and sorting through options in a logical, linear manner to assess the best outcome. This skill is vital for determining things that relate to our physical surroundings and keeping us out of harm's way.

Getting back to the discussion at hand -- how do you determine if something is a judgement or an awareness?

Those just starting out on the consciousness journey often look for the 'what' as a way to tell the difference. They want rules to determine if something is a judgement or not. That would be the "if it is said like this then it is a judgement" kind of rulebook.

If I said "That person is an asshole," it might be a judgement, or it might be an awareness. It is not the statement that determines if it is a judgement. We must take a more in-depth look at the energy delivered with the statement and ask if it locks us up or if it's neutral.

Awareness has a neutral energy. I might be aware when someone is an asshole, the same way I am aware the grass is green or the sky is blue. Let's not get into the actual science of how light refracts and all of that in this book. Let's leave that to the scientists and go with the fact most people do not have judgements of the sky being blue or the grass being green.

A judgement, on the other hand, has a contracted energy to it. It often feels heavy and comes with other energetic attachments. In that case stating, "That person is an asshole," comes with lots of "and that means..." or "and that is wrong because..." -- unspoken tag-alongs that create the judgement energy which then gets stuck in your body.

As people progress with becoming more conscious and letting go of judgements, it gets easier to spot them by the energetic feel the comment carries rather than the words spoken. The statements carry a vibration of their own. Your body feels these vibrations and reacts, giving you vital information your head-brain is not privy to.

Here is where we can take a lesson from our canine friends.

Dogs don't judge. They love unconditionally. Yet, they get their hackles up on first meeting some people. They are smart creatures and often sense things we take longer to clue into or ignore out of a misguided need to be nice or polite. The dog's awareness warns them something is not to be trusted about that person. Trust your dog.

As I free myself of more and more judgement, I am often approached by dogs, and the owners tell me how unusual it is because their dog does not usually approach strangers. I can only assume they sense something in me that feels right to them, that I am safe, or perhaps, they are looking to connect because I am easy to be around. My only issue is I am not a huge fan of dogs. They are cool but give me a cat over a dog any day!

Our bodies can act as finely tuned instruments to guide us to see awareness vs judgements. Our bodies merely respond to the information both spoken and unspoken and give us feedback when we are willing to listen.

## Awareness Muscle Development Exercise

First thing is to get a feel for your internal compass readings. If you are going to use your body as a compass to guide you, then get a feel for what direction or indication says "yes" or "true" for you and which says "no" or "false" for you.

There are many options for tuning in so play around and find a method that works for you. Then roll with it.

**Method 1 - Body Sway**

Stand with your feet hip-width apart.

Out loud or in your mind ask your body to show you a Yes.

Your body should move. Make a note of what direction is "Yes" or "True" for you.

Next, as a double check ask your body to show you a No.

Once you have the directions, play with some questions. For fun, start with things that don't matter or have little significance for you such as:

"Body, would you like a glass of water?"

"Body, would you like a cigarette?"

"Body, would you like a nap?"

"Body, would you like to wear this shirt today?"

Ask questions on a regular basis to get the communication going and connect to your internal knowing.

Your body is being used as a pendulum to provide you with what your gut-brain knows and is trying to tell you.

Ignore any inner voice that says "This is crazy" or that you are making yourself move and it isn't real. You ARE making yourself move. That is the point. However, the nudge to move comes from your inner wisdom, not your cognitive brain.

## Method 2 - Light & Heavy Comparison

This is one that some people struggle to connect to in the beginning, particularly if you are a logical, linear thinker. It will not be rational to your head-brain. Hang in there, though. Even my most resistant, most logical linear thinking client got there in the end.

In this compass comparison, what you are looking for is a sensation in your body to indicate "yes" or "true" vs "no" or "false." Notice what sensations you feel in your body. Ignore your head-brain's attempts to answer the questions and keep your attention on your body instead.

Now, make the statement "My name is (say your real name)."

Notice the sensation, no criticism or judgement simply notice so that you connect to what is true for you.

Next, make the statement "My name is (say a name that is not yours)."

Notice the sensations. It might make you laugh at first since it is a clearly false statement. Do your best to run it a few times so that you tune into your body instead of the humour of the statement.

Here's what to look for: the majority of people have some form of light sensation or open expansive feeling in their body with things that are true, and a heavy, contracted or restrictive sense for things that are false. Your version of light and heavy is perfect however they show up for you.

The important thing here is that you get a gauge on what your personal "light" and "heavy" feel like so you can connect to the intuitive brain (gut-brain) which is NEVER wrong.

I once had a client whose version of light was a tingling in her elbow, and her version of heavy was a tingling in her shoulder. While a most unusual response, it still worked as her internal compass just the same. Once you become familiar with your "true" and "false" compass, you have tapped into the vital information you need to use this energy.

Starting out, stick to things that have less significance for you such as choosing what to wear or what to order from a restaurant. Examples of questions with more significance would be should I take this job or marry this person.

Keep those kinds of check-ins for later when you trust and follow your internal knowing on a regular basis.

As you can imagine the light/heavy knowing is easier to work with day to day since you do not need to be standing to utilize it. For some of the clients I work with, they found the sway test helpful to use for the first couple of months before they tuned into the light/heavy and trusted the sensations they felt.

Eventually, this sensation of awareness will become second nature to you, and you can use it to assess what people tell you. It will become a private lie detector you bring with you everywhere you go.

If you have done a fair bit of prior energy work, you are likely to take to this tool like a fish to water. It can open up a whole new world as you explore what is true and what is false for you.

Ask questions about everything. As you progress, ask about things you are sure are true and areas you have all figured out. Test them to see if they are actually true for you or just something you have been holding on to as right.

For fun, utilize social media to play with this new awareness tool as a "bullshit test." As you are scrolling through the news feed of your favourite social media platform, you can rapidly assess if the post in question is true or false based solely on the energy read (degree of light or heavy feel). Items that carry a strong "heavy" hit in your body are likely spam posts or not the truth from the poster.

You can even let your gaze soften, blurring your vision so that you read only the energy instead of the words. This filters out part of the incoming information so you can focus on the new skill.

Doing a check-in on a post before sharing gives you a new level of information beyond your head-brain. This practice can save you the embarrassment of sharing false news or a post meant to hook people in with emotion.

It also has a second benefit, in that it gives you a level of detachment from what is happening in social media. You become consciously responsive in your actions instead of reactive. Others will see you as an expert instead of another junkie flying off the handle, which enhances your business AND keeps you connected to your Inner Dominatrix.

I use this to quickly filter out who I should add as a Facebook friend and who should be passed over, which dramatically reduces the "You're so beautiful, can we chat" and "come and join my MLM company, you would make so much money" messages. In turn, that creates more ease in my world.

# Chapter 8

# YOUR KINK IS NOT MY KINK

In the world of Kink, there is an ideal that many talk about but few achieve. That is not judging another person's kink as bad just because it is not something you are into.

My dear friend, Anne, who introduced me to this wild and crazy world, was one of those few. She remains curious when she talks to people about what particular flavour of kink they enjoy. She asks questions in a way that gets them to open up and describe what it is about the particular kink or fetish that delights them.

Anne is a cross between a journalist and a charming, innocent child. You just know she loves you and asks out of sheer curiosity. She manages to disarm anyone in her path, and you can't help but open up without a hint of offence at her questions.

It would be so easy to move to revulsion when you encounter something that is a hard limit for you and push the person away energetically and possibly physically. But not Anne. She has learned to lean in and find out more, knowing it does not mean she is in any way required to partake.

I remember her telling me about one such discussion she had with someone who enjoyed drinking the urine of her Master.

For the average person, this would be enough to make your stomach churn and possibly even retch. Even for me, my initial reaction is revulsion, likely because I imagine myself doing it and that kink has no appeal for me.

But digging deeper, we learn that this other submissive, Sarah, experiences this as ultimate surrender and, a way to give herself entirely to her Master. What better way to physically imprint how she gives herself over to him completely, body and soul? Sarah speaks about it being a spiritual experience while at the same time extremely challenging but she is committed to surrendering.

Anne taught me how to get curious. She showed me how to ask questions even when something is foreign and out of my realm. Without trying, she prepped me for my time as a Dominatrix. This preparation allows me to ask questions, set my revulsion aside and learn what exactly a particular kink means to the other person instead of letting my reaction label it wrong.

This did not mean I choose to experience things personally that revolt me, even though Kink is all about pushing your limits and stretching. Some things remain a Hard No (a term used to label types of play that are off limits and will stay off limits).

However, being allowed to peek behind the curtains of what a kink creates for someone, we are invited to let go of our judgement of the act, to see the beauty of it instead. This takes courage. It also takes a willingness to suspend your current perspective.

Being a Dominatrix requires you to dig into that level on a regular basis. Your clients come to you with the belief they are broken or damaged because they have these urges for kinky acts that fall outside the realm of normal or acceptable. It takes tremendous courage for them to open up and admit to you precisely what they are looking for. The last thing they need from a Domme is judgement.

When you are in the initial stage of getting to know them, it is vital to stay open and non-judgemental, so they come to trust you in order to surrender later.

This is the first level of deeply serving your clients. Creating a space where judgement does not exist.

This non-judgemental space is not always easy. At times it will push every button and use every ounce of resolve. It may test your limits, seeing just how committed you are to your chosen path.

The rewards and the internal growth are beyond measure.

As a Dominatrix, letting go of my judgements was not an option, it was a requirement. As a business owner, you would do well to make this a requirement, as well. Getting to the place where you have no judgements about you, your team or your clients, will serve you in ways you cannot imagine.

When a client comes to you with the belief you will create a 50-page website for them for only $500, being free of judgement enables you to respond in a way that shifts their expectations instead of asking if they are smoking crack.

You might say "Tell me what is the most important thing you need your website to do?" Maybe they just have no idea what it takes to build a website and have not considered how much they should invest. Perhaps they have not thought through what they need the site to do, and don't understand they may only need 2 or 3 pages.

Getting more clarity lets, you lead them to "If we created a website that gave you that outcome what increase in income would that mean?" By finding out what is important to them, you can compare the value or ROI to what you would charge.

Asking questions, getting curious, can lead to sales.

Going into judgement leads to foot in mouth disease as you blurt out some flippant remark and lose all possibility of the sale.

The world-at-large functions and thrives on judgement, so your commitment to freeing yourself of judgement will separate you from your competition.

People feel it when you judge them, and they really feel it when you don't. At first, they might be confused because it is so different from the usual way they are treated. But make no mistake. They will be taking note and keep being drawn back to you.

Judgements come in all shapes and sizes. It does not have to be something so dramatic as drinking urine to elicit a critical eye from others. Choice of clothing, hairstyle, where you choose to live, how you talk, how you laugh -- nothing is immune to being judged. And it does not have to be a negative to be a judgement. Someone can see you as attractive, smart or successful but the energy of it is still a judgement.

The tricky part is that it is not the actual thought that makes it a judgement but the energy behind it that creates it. Most people find that concept difficult to comprehend at first.

I suspect I will fail to convey it effectively in written form since energy is at best elusive to the written word. So for the moment, let's move out of the area of business and Kink which can often be filled with emotionally charged judgements and instead let's use nature as a way to connect to this concept.

Tune into what it feels like to look up at the sky and observe how it looks without thinking "this means we have this kind or that of weather." Merely observe the colour and the textures, or lack of textures, in the sky. Just notice. Expand out and drop more into noticing without any need to make it mean anything.

Ideally, you will have experienced non-judgement.

If you felt a sense of ease in your body, a feeling of spaciousness and neutrality of emotion then well done. You tapped into the experience I was hoping you would.

No doubt you are well and truly familiar with the feeling of judgement. I have yet to meet anyone who has gone through life without experiencing it from both sides of that fence. However, just for fun, think of someone with whom you do not agree with their choices. If you don't know anyone close to you, politicians are an easy target.

Think about what you don't agree with. Think about how you think they should change.

I would be willing to bet you are feeling constricted in your body, possibly getting angry. How is your heart rate? A little elevated? Depending on the intensity of the judgement you will experience these sensations on a range. The more intense the judgement, the more intense the physical reaction.

Loads of fun for you and your body. Not!

This brief experiment gives you a glimpse into the physical benefits you gain by giving up judgement. You have more freedom in your body and more ease moving through life.

You will also give others this same kind of space and ease. That is an incredible gift which is a big part of why it is so appealing for your team and your clients to be around you when you practice non-judgement.

As a business owner, it is not about feeling good and singing Kumbaya. You still need to helm the ship and make things happen. And lucky for you, removing the judgements has a massive impact on your ability to do both.

When you are stuck in a judgement of yourself, then you are likely doubting your abilities. That may mean you're not as productive as you could be. That results in the ever-so-helpful bullshit stories about how you can't do it, or why you shouldn't or who will say what if you do.

That, my friend, is the hamster wheel. Spinning fast but going nowhere.

Those internal judgements of yourself keep you stuck and non-productive. They cost you revenue. How is that for hitting where it hurts? Yes, your judgements repel money.

If the money doesn't motivate you, then look at the cost of time and energy. How much time are you spending on this loop? How much does it drain you? You could be out for a walk, soaking up the sunshine but instead you are spinning on the wheel, wearing yourself out.

That sucks!

And for what? Judgements?

Are they really so precious you are unwilling to dig them out? I could swear they are a precious metal the way some people are bound and determined to hang on to them. They act like they are manna from heaven or something!

When you give up judging yourself, I promise you will make faster decisions and feel less anxiety about your work. You will discover more fun in what you do, and if not, you will likely change to something that is fun.

Being in business is work so you might as well be doing something you have fun with.

That is where I find the wisdom in the expression "Do what you love, and the money will follow." It is not the whole Law of Attraction thing here, but rather, do what makes your heart sing because it gives you the drive to dig in day after day and show up when others have long since quit. That is when the money comes in. Eventually, people notice, and things roll.

When I started down this path with the Dominatrix thing, it seemed like no one wanted to have anything to do with me. People were not sure what I was selling, or why I would bother to bring something so controversial into the business world. They told me I was limiting my options instead of expanding them.

I tried retreating and using a creative play on words with 'PowerNatrix' for a bit, but that was not me being entirely authentic. I was holding back, judging myself.

I still had clients - thanks to getting incredible results – however, business was not coming in in the volume I knew it could be.

Once I finally surrendered fully into this theme and said to hell with what a few people thought, my business took off. I welcomed the naysayers to get on board or move out of my way.

Slowly at first, but steadily I saw a shift from me reaching out to appear on shows to shows reaching out to me. My group programs filled up with a third of the effort it took before, and engagement went up on my social media.

When I stopped doing this for others approval, I started doing it for the joy of creating change in peoples' lives. I let go of measuring my success by the money coming in and instead celebrated every thank you, every testimonial, and every opportunity.

It was time for me to put the tools I taught to the ultimate test - being ALL in!

Just like in the Dungeon, I entirely focused on doing what needed to be done. My attitude became "Screw the distractions." I got into the energy of my Inner Dominatrix instead.

It is not quite the same high I got from a session, but it is an incredible ride, none the less. Well worth every ounce of energy I put toward removing the judgements and being free!

The same can be true for you.

## How to Get Rid of the Judgements

I am going to assume I have your buy-in that this is worth your time and energy, so let's look at some tools. What exactly will it take for you to get free?

First, let me warn you that few people make this work through a self-help style program. It is the very rare individual who can find on their own what they have been avoiding looking at.

The obvious judgements are easy to address. Then there are the ones you are oh, so attached to; the ones you absolutely know you are right about. These are the judgements and beliefs likely to trip you up -- if you even look at them at all.

However, if you are determined to brave this on your own, then grab a friend - one whom you trust to be honest - and commit to working through the layers together. There is nothing quite so powerful as someone else calling you on your bullshit.

Be aware. If you are both new, there is a danger one or both of you will be easily triggered. It's not easy to hold the space of no-judgement when calling each other on your shit.

Move into this with full awareness so that you don't end up hating your friend.

Judgements are stored energetically in our bodies and can be released with your intention to release them.

This is what I see most new people do: they grab hold of 5% (or even 10%) of the judgement and the stuff related to it and only let go of that. Then they wonder why they still feel stuck. That's because the other 90-95% is still there. The majority of it!

When you dig into this work, there needs to be a willingness to really let it go. Without that surrender all energy tools and psychotherapy tools are useless.

It is like that old joke. How many psychiatrists does it take to change a light bulb?

One - but the light bulb must want to change.

Lots of people tell me they want their life to change, but when I get rooting around in what they need to let go of to have the outcome they want...well, then it becomes a different story. Suddenly, they offer a million reasons about why they need to hang on to being right.

It takes courage to go against the grain and give up all your judgements. How do you define yourself? How do you determine who a good person is? How do you figure out where you stand?

You will need to be willing to be uncomfortable and ready to stand on the edge of the abyss to grab the reward of ultimate ease and surrender to who you are. Who you really are!

This process is the same regardless of what the judgement is about.

Grab hold of that judgement energy. Pull it out of your system and throw it in a pile. Look for deeper layers and pull those out. Repeat until you feel a sense of ease in your body accompanied by an awareness you have pulled out as much as you possibly can at this moment. Then choose to blast it. Destroy it to keep it from returning.

This is not about speed. It is about being thorough. The more deeply you connect to all the tentacles or related energetic threads the more you remove.

Think of pulling dandelions from your lawn. Gawd knows I have dug out enough of those suckers over the years. If you pluck only the heads of the flowers off the plant that is like removing 10% of the judgement. The roots remain, the dandelion keeps growing and produces more flowers.

Most people keep plucking flowers hoping to kill the weed.

Some people get more aggressive and pull on the weed and grab everything visible above ground. While this provides more relief, there is still that tap root underground, slowly re-growing. Perhaps not as large but it is still there.

It's only by using one of those handy garden tools that you get the whole taproot. Now you have eliminated the source, and it will not come back.

If you have ever gone organic with your lawn you understand this truth - once you remove the weeds, you must keep an eye out for new seedlings. While this is an on-going process, it is easier to maintain than fix once it is overgrown.

It's the same idea with using the energy tools to remove the judgements. The tool helps you to get to the root when applied correctly. You want to go deep to get the whole root.

# Chapter 9

# THE JOY OF THE PAIN

We are going to move to the other side of the whip for a moment, learning valuable lessons and insights from the submissive side of things. As a Dominatrix, it is vital for you to understand what the submissive is experiencing so that you are better able to control the scene and create an outcome that is in their best interests.

As a business owner, you can utilize the counterbalance of the submissive energy. This allows you to engage all possible tools and tricks to fast track your success with minimal stress on you and your body.

While the Dominatrix may hold the whip, the submissive still holds the ultimate power to stop the scene. It is a consensual role play on both parts while the reality is each role is dynamic and interdependent on the other for both to grow.

You as a business owner will have times you need to hold the space in a Dominatrix style, AND you will need to lean into the submissive and her gift of powerful surrender.

## The Pleasure is All Mine

In the world of BDSM, pain is something experienced as erotic and enjoyable. The pain allows the surrender and release, even profound spiritual transformation and awakening.

If you have not been part of this world that probably seems crazy. How could someone possibly find pain erotic?

Let me start by stating what is obvious in the Kink world - that there is pleasure-pain and there is pain-pain. Even one who identifies as a masochist will not enjoy breaking a leg or even stubbing their toe.

However, in the scene, things are set up in such a way that pain becomes pleasurable. Anticipation starts well before the actual scene commences so by the time the scene starts a good dose of endorphins are racing through the body. This signals the brain that something delightful is coming.

Then the scene slowly ramps up, gradually increasing the pain techniques interspersed with pleasure to keep the brain releasing the internal chemicals that allow one to surrender and enjoy the moment.

Let me take you to the Dungeon for a moment so you can "see" how this works.

The submissive has ankle and wrist restraints attached to a standing apparatus that looks like a large leaning X of solid wood. Each of the cuffs latched on to anchor points at each of the four points of the cross, and the body can be supported by the apparatus. The submissive has limited freedom of movement. Just enough so they can enjoy the struggle.

With the submissive secured in place, we can begin the "torture" session. We start with some light touch to connect. Perhaps dragging your fingernails down the back with enough force to leave a delicious red mark on the blank canvas before you.

Next, we play with the mental aspect of this game, cracking the whip in the air to make noise without hitting the submissive. If you have built the anticipatory tension, your submissive will flinch at the sound, which creates even more tension as they wait for the initial strike.

The first strike is somewhat light, although strong enough to be unmistakably felt by the submissive. You watch their reaction so you can gauge how to land the next strike. After a brief period with the whip, you switch back to the light touch.

The nerve endings in the skin are on high alert so this light sensation will be intense although different. The rest period allows the body time to release the endorphins and to perceive the last round as a base level.

With each round, the force of the whip is gradually increased based on the response from the submissive. You keep watching for clues to make it painful without bringing them out of the delicious trance state. Each round is intended to take them deeper into the trance, release more endorphins and push them past their imagined limitations into deep surrender.

Finally, the submissive is released from the constraints and allowed time to integrate the session.

If the intensity is ramped up too quickly the submissive does not drop into that sweet subspace. They miss out on the pleasure side of the pain and only experience the pain. When the pain intensity is applied to heavily too soon, the submissive is jarred into a state of experiencing pain-pain. Like stubbing your toe, it jolts you out of whatever you were engaged in.

As a Dominatrix, this is a terrible business plan, considering that pain and only pain does not keep people coming back begging for more. The strategic application of a gradual ramping up interspersed with rest that allows the body to adjust and create the heady concoction leading to deep surrender and release.

Sub-space (a trance-like state created by a good BDSM scene) is the best high you could imagine -- profoundly aware and in your body while totally blissed out and devoid of a care in the world. The added bonus being that the side effects are releasing your past baggage and limitations.

When we enter a state of trance, we access our subconscious mind directly. When a scene is created to stir up old memories and traumas intentionally, we retrieve the subconscious programming initially installed on our internal hard drive. This allows us to change it to a more empowering and helpful program.

Let me explain how this works.

When we look at the scientific research on pain and pleasure, we find a number of overlapping systems that affect how we process these things within the brain. When we experience a sensation in the body, it is up to the brain (primarily the brain stem area) to process that sensation and inform us as to what kind of sensation it is.

For example, when we burn our finger on the stove, our body tells us that is pain. If the information does not get to the brain from the finger, like with a person whose nerves have been damaged, the sensation of pain is not registered. There is a risk of severe damage because the reflex to pull back is not activated.

This leaves some flexibility for the brain to rewire or re-identify what is pain and what is pleasure, leaving it possible to experience pain as pleasure and vice versa. For example, hot wax dripped onto the body, while painful, can also be interpreted by the brain as pleasure during a scene.

When I think back to when my sister gave birth to her daughter, I am still astounded at how high her pain tolerance was. She talked me into providing support and to do massage on her during the labour pains.

Let me tell you, that was the most physically intense work I have ever done as a massage therapist and yet she said she could barely feel it. I was a therapist known for deep work and normally when I treated her I had to keep backing off. And yet, in this case, there was no way for me to apply enough pressure.

Her response to pain changed due to the flood of internal chemicals preparing her body for birth. This is quite incredible and demonstrates we are capable of going through intense experiences. Because of the amazing machine our bodies are, we barely feel it, or at least do not perceive it as pain. When we go through an extreme situation like birth, the body floods with endorphins, the body's natural painkillers.

This great system kicks in so you can override pain and get out of dangerous situations (along with some help from adrenaline). Thankfully, it kicks in during childbirth, or the human race would never have survived. No woman would have endured that amount of pain to have another child.

This is the same chemistry that kicks in with BDSM. With some help from Mother Nature and some strategic methods for applying the pain during a 'scene,' the person receiving the whipping can surrender into the pain and allow it to transform them.

If we look to the sports world, you see countless examples of people who push themselves to extremes to excel at their sport. The intensity of the training that is endured to get to the level of pro or Olympic athlete is incredible.

Conditioned to push through the pain, high-level athletes challenge their bodies to push past limits and reach a new performance norm. Countless numbers carry on performing despite injuries. I watched a performance where a figure skater sliced their calf during a competition and yet managed to finish the routine.

I don't know about you, but they would have been taking me out on a stretcher if I had that injury. I would not have continued skating. No way!

For these athletes, the competition and the goal are so firmly etched in their minds, there is no stopping for pain. They use it to work for them instead of against them.

Marathon runners are a fantastic example of this. There is a point where they "hit the wall," feeling like they can't go on. The experienced runners know this is just a phase and lean into that pain to finish the race in spite of it, making the victory all the sweeter. They also have incredibly high amounts of endorphins and adrenaline pumping through their veins during the competition. They do not feel the pain until later, thus explaining how they could possibly push through to finish their competition regardless of their injuries.

Back to the Dungeon.

The pain coupled with the pleasure and erotic excitement changes the perception of the pain and how it is perceived in the body. The intensity of pain delivered is slowly ramped up. Each round of spanking is more intense than the last, so the changes in the body have time to take place, allowing the submissive to receive more.

The slow ramp-up drives up the endorphins in the body, changing the signals to the brain. Then, when the pain is intermixed with some soft, often sensual touching, the contrast in sensations again revs up the body chemistry, enabling it to take more and more.

Now, before this turns into a BDSM sexy tale, let's get back on track.

In business, there are going to be many tough challenges to deal with - aka the "pain" of being in business. There will be days when it feels like the whole world is against you, that people do not understand who you are and what you are trying to do. There will also be numerous setbacks, financial failures, or people who rip off your ideas or creations.

To be successful, just like the marathon runner you need to lean into that pain and keep going. Being in business is not for the faint at heart. It takes courage every step of the way, and you need tools and tricks to make it easier to keep going despite the setbacks and obstacles.

In an ideal world, I would recommend taking some time before starting your business to clear out a good chunk of your emotional baggage and beliefs that keep you from moving forward. (See the appendix for the tools). You will likely never be completely free from baggage but free enough that challenges do not trigger you into victim mode again.

If you did not take the time before beginning this journey, it is not too late. Get some help to move through it as fast as possible so you can get back to taking strategic action and moving forward again.

There are a plethora of books on the market to walk you through the process of releasing your baggage. Personally, I believe hiring a good life coach or energy healer to be the quickest and most effective route for lasting change. Pick one known for results. You are looking for change, not to make a new friend.

A client of mine was creating a tech start-up company with her husband, but she had this running story of how much they were bootstrapping the business to get it going. While that was true and necessary, three years later, the story stopped serving her. She projected a "slice of whine" with that story every time she told it.

The energy behind her words repelled the investors with more money they were hoping to attract. They saw where she was stuck. Concerned about the ROI, they would take a pass on this incredible opportunity.

I worked with her to remove the whine produced by the energetic imprint that three years of scraping by had created for her and the company. Once we released the programs from her system, she saw options for utilizing the funds they had and freed up funds so she could purchase a vehicle again. Each time she slid behind the wheel of her shiny new ride pulled her out of "feeling poor."

This made a dramatic impact on the business, they drew in more prominent investors and more opportunities because they could confidently drive to them.

Changing things internally allows us to take bigger, bolder action in our own business, bringing in more clients and more money. Each time you up-level, which could be taking on a new team member to help your business, a new project or a growth in sales, you are going to want to have someone to work with to bust through the resistance. Each up-level brings forth a new level of resistance to clear out.

There will also be bigger challenges and issues for you to deal with which requires faster decisions to keep your business running smoothly. Keep expanding your personal emotional bandwidth so you can expand your business.

Growing a business is often as much of a personal growth and development journey as it is about expanding your reach, income and impact. I watch my clients experience this exciting shift as they become more visible, generate more business and bring in more money.

However, I've also noticed a tipping point where people come out of the woodwork to say nasty things about you and your work. The exact moment this happens is different for everyone.

For example, with Facebook, there seems to be a tipping point around 1000 followers when the first of the "haters" pop their heads up and post hurtful comments on your wall or in response to your posts. The initial reaction for most people is to retreat and reduce the behaviour creating this backlash. The problem, of course, is that cutting back on posting only hurts you financially.

We need to thicken our skin to these types of people and move forward in spite of them. This is where personal growth happens. You must learn not to allow what they think to affect or impact you. You need to recognize what self-judgements or self-defeating programs they triggered and then dig in and remove those from your system.

When you have done a complete removal of those beliefs, you will welcome the rude or hateful comments as evidence of your success. They become milestone markers. When you can celebrate someone cyber-stalking you, you will know you have mastered this thickened skin and detachment energy.

These incidents will fuel your business instead of your emotions. Once you have done your foundational work and released any traumas from your body, you can play with the energy of your Inner Dominatrix. This work liberates the power and willingness to lead in your business.

It continues to amaze me how this process frees people up to sidestep challenges with ease. Not clearing this up, I can safely predict struggle and frustration on a regular basis with your business. Even if you are not admitting it, those underlying issues trigger your emotional response. That emotional response keeps you from taking action.

Leading from your Inner Dominatrix blends the energy of serving deeply (being client-centred), the willingness to hold the power (stand in your expertise) and taking control of the scene (moving into action).

Again, using social media, for example, this power shows up as easily letting people know what your expertise is. You will no longer downplay it but allow yourself to get excited about what you do. You become an invitation for your ideal clients to play in your world by standing firmly in what you do for them and sharing your ability to assist them if they are ready. You easily create posts that add value to who they are and what they need and consistently show up so they can find you.

When you are willing to run your business from the Inner Dominatrix people will swoop in from miles around. They want what you are offering merely because they are drawn to your magnetic energy. They can't help themselves in much the same way a submissive swoons for the Domme in the room.

There is no faking this energy, showing up authentically as your Inner Dominatrix, it needs to be integrated with who you are. This is a journey and not an overnight flip of a switch.

The more you release your self-judgements, labels and definitions of who you are, the more you are ready to hold the Inner Dominatrix energy. Lean into her. Trust her. In the end, she is you.

Trust your intuitive knowing and be willing to follow it in all areas of your life. Gradually, that power and strength will build, and you can use it to ask for the bigger sale, reach out to leaders for a connection or joint venture, and even raise your rates in line with what is required for your business to succeed.

Just as the submissive demands of the Domme to own their power, so in business you must step in fully if you want to lead effectively.

This Dominatrix energy does not mean you become pushy and bossy. Remember that one of the keys to this energy is also about serving deeply.

This client-centred focus extends out to treating every member of your team with the same care and compassion as your clients. After all, how you treat your team is how they will treat the clients.

Go into any business, and you can quickly see if the company leads from a "power with" or a "power over" mindset simply by your interactions with their front-line staff.

If the majority of the front-line staff are rude or apathetic about you as the customer, I guarantee the leadership is more dictatorship than collaborative. When front-line staff have no voice in a company and the leaders do not value or appreciate them, they inevitably dole that attitude out on the customers in turn.

Compare that to the experience of going into a Starbucks cafe. Almost every store I have been in around the world (save for the airport ones which are not corporate run) the staff are friendly. They seem to enjoy their work and take pride in the company. I know baristas and managers of various locations, and I can vouch for the fact that the Starbucks Corporation listens to their front-line staff. They value them and take steps to make them feel included and appreciated. In turn, the staff showers that attitude on the customers.

Taking a step back and asking yourself, "How can I come from the place of serving deeply?" allows you to take inspired action.

For me, this showed up in the early days of moving my business to a coaching model and running webinars. I saw that I could create massive transformations for my clients yet I held on to the idea they "should" just hire me because I was so talented. Some days, I look back and think it is incredible I was as busy as I was, given my underlying attitude. However, as I dropped into making service my focus instead of how much I was making, I drew in more clients.

This is not to say I was not aware of the money or neglecting it. However, when it came to client work, the accounting hat was put in the closet. I focused on deeply serving the client right in front of me, pushing out all the other details and responsibilities.

When it came time to plan or review my business, then the CEO and accountant came out to play, making sure that the rates and offerings lined up, so the business remained profitable.

If you have not yet dug into your business numbers, you need to do that. Even if someone else does your accounting and bookkeeping, you must know how to evaluate and keep an eye on the financial health of your business. If you aren't aware of what is going on with your money, then someone could be slipping things past you.

Money is an emotional minefield for most people. You think you are okay and then suddenly, something happens. You get triggered into feeling fear about money or worrying that there will not be enough.

We then pile on all the cultural and religious ideas and judgements about money. Is it any wonder the majority of people are in a financial mess with their businesses?

Most of us are not taught about money; how to handle it, how to make it work for us and how to get it to grow. Mysteriously we are somehow supposed to just "know" what to do with it. That's crazy.

Learn about money; learn about how it works and how to make it work for you. Learn how to read your financial statements and how to manage your books even if you hire out. These skills are vital in business, yet I am shocked at how many entrepreneurs are in a financial mess because they play ostrich with it.

This is not the book to discuss the specifics of money; however, the world is not lacking in great resources. One of my favourites is Suzie Orman's The Courage to Be Rich. *Side Note: Stay Tuned for next book; The Inner Dominatrix Guide To: Badass Abundance, that will dive into all things money related.

## Success Stories!

*My definition of success is always changing, unfolding, evolving. At one time success was merely getting by, putting food on the table as a single mum … later it became being self employed as a healer when people weren't making careers out of that … at another time it was having the Reiki seat invented for me at BNI.*

*In 2006, I was visiting a BNI to see if what I did would be well received by business professionals. Dana came up to me and said, "the world needs you and someone who can articulate the healing arts as well as you do." I got the reputation as "the non-flakey Reiki lady" and the rest was history.*

*Well, not really, the history is still being written. Dana became a trusted friend and mentor, to this day she is one of the few people who can call me on my sh\*t. Who trusts me enough to work on her when she needs it, and pushes me to always be more that who or what I think I am.*

*She knocked conventional energy work on its ear, it was probably from her that I learned to expand out; really that makes so much more sense than shielding or contracting and protecting. She taught me to ask my body if what I was hearing in my thoughts or felt in my body was mine or something else. I expanded my repertoire of healing modalities under her tutelage. I learned I was more powerful than I even wanted to be, and to step into "my big girl panties" and take on the world.*

*I'm not sure I would have taken on 36 speaking engagements every year without Dana helping me see my greater vision and influence… follow the energy. It wasn't what we were working on specifically; I just uncovered my truth, got out of my own way, and followed the energy.*

~Jessy Morrison – *www.jessymorrison.ca*

# Finding the Fun in the Pain

We all have things that are less than joyful when it comes to business, and yet you have a choice. You have the option to do it or not do it. But when it comes to things you really need to get done to achieve your long-term goals, then you must dig in and get it done.

However, when we do things we do not enjoy and tell ourselves that we "have to," we set ourselves up to hate the task. Then, if you are like me, your inner rebel kicks in, and you avoid and distract yourself. Suddenly the dishes really need you to wash them.

So, when it comes to those tasks or projects that must get done, and you are not able to delegate them out, your choice becomes:

Do it while grumbling and hating it

Or

Find a way to make it fun.

I can hear the resistance. You are saying "But 'xyz' is never fun."

Well, if you refuse to even consider how it could be fun, then you will never find the fun. Let me assure you, there is always a way to sneak in at least a sliver of joy to anything you do.

Ask yourself questions to open up the creative juices and get them flowing. The simple act of asking "How can I make this fun?" engages your brain to look for ways to make it more enjoyable.

It does not have to be anything significant. It can be as simple as putting on some great music while you do your books or grabbing a mug of your favourite tea to enjoy while you make your To-Do list. Taking the edge off your task begins to shift things around.

You know that time flies when you are having fun, so if you find creative ways to make those Have-To-Do's more enjoyable, they will be over and done with before you know it.

You can even make a game out of it. If you are the highly competitive type and you have a project or task to tackle, pit yourself against the clock. Make it a race to complete your assignment before the alarm goes off.

Be reasonable, however. If you are submitting a trademark application, then a one-hour alarm is only going to add stress to the situation. God knows government forms are the driest of the dry and can be a confusing process unless you do them all the time. On the other hand, giving yourself twenty minutes to craft an email to your list will likely provide the perfect push to get it done and not over think it.

Remember - your head-brain will go looking for answers to the questions you ask of it.

This means that if you ask, "Why does this suck?" then your head-brain, like the obedient little golden retriever it is, will show you all the reasons why it sucks. It will pull out the encyclopedic evidence stored over the years to prove to you that you suck or "it" sucks. You have seen this in action enough to know how skilled your lovely brain is at finding this kind of confirmation.

Turn your Why question around to work for you and ask, "I wonder why this is so easy and fun for me?" Now your golden retriever goes running off to fetch that particular stick of information for you.

Keep in mind this is likely a new game for your brain so, if the information is slow or seemingly non-existent at first, keep with it. It works!

Each time you ask yourself, "I wonder why this is so easy and fun for me?" your brain lays down new neuropathways. Sure, it takes time. Just like summer road construction, it may be frustratingly slow but well worth it in the end.

There is also the trick of turning your task into a game by adding something fun to it. One of the things I do to make cleaning the house a neutral task is to grab the iPad and put on a show or a movie to watch while I work. This does triple duty with guilt-free TV time while I get things done and I am moving.

Podcasts are also great for cleaning. (Have you subscribed to mine yet? – Inner Dominatrix found on all Podcast subscription platforms)

They are easier to access as you do not have to be in view of the screen like with TV shows plus there is such a wide variety available now to choose from. Any topic you can imagine has a podcast you can dig into. There are even modern versions of old-time radio shows to stimulate a different part of your brain and activate your imagination.

**The Dominatrix tricks are:**

1. How can this be fun?

2. How can I get someone else to do it for me?

This may be hiring someone, finding a volunteer or someone who is willing to trade with you for services. The more often you ask the question, the more options you open yourself to.

# Chapter 10

# DIG IN - IT FEELS GOOD!

Over the last 100 years, as society has invented more gadgets and gizmos to make our lives easier, we may have lost touch with how good it feels to dig in and work hard. We can have food in five minutes with microwaves. We can throw our dirty clothes into a machine and walk away while it does the work. We have cars to take us swiftly to our destinations.

I am all for those gadgets. I would not want to give up my washing machine or vacuum - although I would love someone else to run them. And let's not even consider giving up my car! I love zipping around. The feeling of freedom I derive from driving remains with me since I first got my driver's license at 16.

If I did my cleaning by hand or walked everywhere I needed to go, I would not have time to do what I am most passionate about, so I am quite grateful for the conveniences. However, with all these great devices and the shift to all things computerized we have taken our society to a place of minimal activity compared to just a century ago.

We now must intentionally add in exercise to get the movement our bodies require. Movement which would have been part of our normal day-to-day activities not that long ago is missing today.

Being inactive is worse for our health than smoking, which means that a smoker who is regularly exercising is healthier than a non-smoker who is a thin couch potato. The first time I heard that I was shocked. I always thought of smoking as very bad but apparently, spending all day on my laptop is worse than a pack of smokes - who knew!

I recently bought one of those fitness tracker devices to encourage myself to break up my time at the computer and move more. I found something rather sad in this. Sad that I am paying money to do something that is or should be natural.

When I look around at the world at large, I see a general lack of willingness to dig into things that are hard. People want to collect a paycheck with the least amount of effort possible. There is a constant cry for easier, faster. This sets us up to fall prey to the schemers out there promising the easy or fast buck.

In business, there are so many claims that this program or that seminar will get you "6 Figures in 60 Days" or a no-fail, super-easy way to make your first Million. The fast-talking sales pitches and those well-crafted landing pages are like the call of the siren leading our bank balances to crash on rocky shores.

When you look for easy, you are set up to jump on these bandwagons and swiftly throw several thousand on the latest credit card, expecting you will make the money back before the card is due.

Well, how has that worked out?

I recall a time in my early 20's I went to one of "those" seminars.

You know the kind I am talking about. The glossy ad promising big money and all the perks only available to travel agents and unbelievably "all while working part-time." After driving over an hour to get to the venue, I then stood in line with all the other suckers who had been drawn in for the evening.

As we waited for the doors to open, people chatted and joked with each other with an undertone of nervousness. There was an element of the unknown here. Most had never done one of these things before and were not sure what it was about, but everyone shared a desire to make hordes of easy money.

Finally, allowed to enter the hallowed hall, we were ushered into the seats to watch the Greatest Show on Earth. Or at least you would have thought that was what you were watching when you saw how excited the presenters were about the product they flogged from the stage.

I was captivated, sucked into every word. YES! I wanted free travel! YES! I wanted to make $10K a month from this super easy system!

YES! YES! YES!

When they finally announced they were taking signups at the back, I was so in! I jumped up and, in my excitement to rush to the back, I stepped on a few toes of the wiser participants in my aisle who stayed seated. I was not going to miss out on the super-fast action bonuses!

I pulled out my credit card and charged the $2,000 to get my package. I was pumped! I was going to rock this.

That excitement lasted all the way home as I dreamt of all the things I would buy with the money I would make. How easy my life was going to be. And of course, let's not forget all the places I would travel to for super cheap.

When I got home, I contacted a few of my friends to tell them about this new travel package I was selling and how they could save on their hotels and airfare by buying the deal. I had a few who were genuinely interested. This was going great!

Then I started to look at the details of the package I was selling. I began to see the fine print and the restrictions. Slowly it sank in that what I had purchased and what I was selling was not the great deal I thought. These discounts were not that fantastic, after all.

As the sparkle faded from my shiny new program, the truth hit me full force. I had just been sucked in.

I packed up that package and all the brochures and holders and tucked them in the corner of my closet. I never mentioned it again to any of my friends. I prayed they would not ask me about it so I would not have to own up to the fact I was a sucker.

I left that package in the closet to torment myself for a good two years - which was about how long it took me to pay off my credit card. Two years of working a bit extra each week to chip away at the interest and principal on the card. This was back in the days of only having an income from my massage practice, so I physically worked my ass off to pay back that money.

I did not say anything to anyone about this mistake or the pain of paying off that card. One day, when I finally had enough of looking at those stupid brochures, I threw them out. The learning, however, profoundly stuck with me and I am very grateful the lesson was not more expensive or more painful. I am also thankful that I never actually sold any of those packages since they were not all they were cracked up to be.

I really wish I could say that experience taught me to let go of chasing lottery-type wins or easy money but sadly it did not. It does prevent me from going to any of these types of seminars again, which is significant.

So when those Money Mindset free seminars come to town, I have no trouble saying NO because I understand the set up is to push you hard for 12 hours a day, cram your brain with information to tire you so they can brainwash you into spending big money at the back of the room.

No thanks!

It's good that I can laugh at myself now. It is also good I detached from the belief that making money is something significant and heavy.

I can honestly say that giving up the lottery mentality, where I looked for "easy and quick" has been the best thing I did for myself, and it enabled me to make more money. By not focusing on money, I shifted my focus to the things I need to do to grow my business and serve my tribe in a big way. Things like engaging with people in my Facebook group without expecting them to spend money with me. Investing in systems to make things easier for my clients – not just what is easiest for me.

That is my success secret - hard work that is strategic and consistent.

The thing is this. It is fun! I enjoy digging in because I want to dig in because I want to serve more. If you follow the Law of Attraction, you understand that joy and fun is what pulls in people. For me, those are the people who spend money on my programs and books. (Thanks for buying this one by the way).

When you view the effort required to run your business as an exciting challenge instead of a chore, things shift and open up for you. Playing with the question "How can I make this more fun?" is helpful for tasks like paperwork or bookkeeping.

You can always find a way to make what you are doing more fun. Our brains are incredible tools, provided we put them to good use. Your brain is at your command, your submissive if you step into your Inner Dominatrix and take charge.

The logical brain is fantastic at calculating mathematical equations, mapping out routes, or even summarizing things for reports. It is not the best at coming up with creative new solutions. Your heart-brain and your gut-brain are skilled at those tasks.

Remember that when you ask your head-brain for solutions, it will search the database and archives for something similar and give you an answer based on the past. Maybe this will be helpful, but more often than not it is an old outdated solution that will not work. For example... telling yourself "this task sucks, or I always mess up when doing my taxes."

Coming up with new inspired ideas of making the task fun requires you to drop down into your body to check in with the heart and the gut. Sit with the challenge until an idea on how to make it fun pops up, or let it percolate while you go off and do other things. Allow the inspiration to jump up when you are least expecting it.

If your logical brain needs a job, give it this question "Why is it so easy for me to have fun with this?" Asking Why questions send your mind on a mission to compile the evidence.

This can either be dangerous or helpful to you, depending on the question you ask. If you ask a question like "Why am I so fucked up?" the brain goes right to work listing out all the things you have done wrong since you were two years old, happily documenting all the evidence to support your question.

However, when we ask questions like "Why is this so fun?" the mind works for you instead of against you, making it your submissive.

For a more in-depth look at the use of Why questions to create change, check out Affirmations by Noah St. John.

The principle is to turn your affirmation into a Why statement to make it more effective as described above.

Digging in is not about making all of it fun. It's also about pushing through bigger challenges.

I suspect part of the appeal to experience a session with a Dominatrix is that desire on the part of the submissive to physically push through something challenging; to grapple with forces out of their control and to survive; to etch in deeply the strength they need to withstand whatever life throws at them.

If you ever have been through what I would call mild life-threatening experiences you understand what I am talking about. Especially if it happens to have been an experience shared with a number of people.

One summer we were at the Yacht Club to watch the fireworks on Canada Day. Usually, we would have gone out on the boat and observed from the water, but the weather did not look good. We chose to stay on land.

Not everyone made that choice. Many of the boaters came into town early in the morning to anchor for the festivities and enjoy the day.

That year, a fierce storm with strong winds and torrential rains broke just as the fireworks were going off.

Those of us already on shore ran out in the downpour to assist boats seeking safety inside the harbour. The storm was strong enough to make us afraid for the safety of the boaters. It also brought out the best of humanity at that moment. People left their dry shelter to rescue strangers in need.

As the storm eased and the rescued boats got underway once again, the energy was electric among everyone at the club. The shared experience of pushing through something scary and doing it together was incredible. Even those who stayed inside were caught up in the excitement.

I felt amazed at how it allowed people to bond and drop the usual pretences, seeing one another as equal. Laughter rang out, and our hearts overflowed as a result of that shared effort. We were having so much fun celebrating the victory, there was no rush to leave and get back to our homes to dry off.

We recounted our moments in the storm, laughing about how soaked we were and the mishaps and slips of this person or that on the way out. Even now, as I write these words, I can step back into that feeling, letting it wash over and envelop me once again.

Something magical happens when people encounter threats together, be it big events like the 9-11 aftermath and the outpouring of volunteers, or smaller things like my Canada Day storm. We get something out of pushing through and overcoming that can be quite motivating.

Perhaps we need to intentionally put more challenges in place, so we feel that high more often, instead of looking for it to be more comfortable. Join a boot camp, climb the CN Tower, run a race or a marathon. Those tests will give you a taste of that high, the elation of pushing through. Then bring that energy back to your business and use it to push through the resistance of whatever you are currently encountering.

The lure for life to be easy is strong. Going against that inclination to surrender to the 'pain' of your business challenges requires you to become your own Domme. Push your limits and praise your success.

Physically challenging activities such as weight training, running a race, or entering a dance competition are ideal for this training. They give you that pleasure-pain opportunity. You could tell yourself that "This is hard, and it sucks," or you could lean in and connect with the incremental changes in your body's strength. Push past the mental chatter and move, in spite of that noise in your head.

While you can hire a personal trainer to push you, at some point, you need to acquire that skill for yourself. You want that Inner Dominatrix energy available to you 24/7 so you can lean into it as the challenges come along.

Here is your first challenge, should you choose to accept it:

Start your day with that cold shower that we looked at in the 'What Fucking Comfort Zone' chapter.

Force yourself to shower only in cold water. This is you Domming you. You are likely going to tell yourself that it will suck and that it will be hard. Ignore those voices because when you are done, you will have a sense of accomplishment and survival that pumps you up for the day.

If you need to ease into it, start hot and finish the last 3 min with cold. If you run cold normally, this will have you feeling warmer for the rest of the day as your body works to react to the burst of cold.

On the off chance you happen to be an extremist and love a full-out challenge, then Google "The Ice Man" to learn about his system of breathing and mind control. It enables him to be in icy cold water or outside in frigid temperatures without feeling the effects of the cold on his body. His immune system and that of his trainees have been medically proven to be off the charts. I find it fascinating and on the list of possible future experiences.

There is, of course, the added bonus that a cold shower boosts your immune system - which you need for running your business. You can't afford to be sick.

Research shows us that cold showers:

- Build strong willpower

- Improve emotional resiliency

- Improve immunity and circulation

- Increase alertness - better than coffee for jolting you awake and stimulating your brain

- Stimulate weight loss

- Ease stress

- Speed up muscle recovery

- Relieve depression.

Your exercise routine is another area to implement this 'Domming You' approach. Push yourself to do just 5 more, be it 5 more minutes or 5 more reps. Push past that point where you usually stop.

"Domming You" is an incredible tool that rewires your brain. It trains you to rise to the challenges bound to pop up in your business instead of shrinking from them.

When faced with a list of prospect calls, this rewiring changes the thought pattern of "I can't do anymore" to "I can do 5 more calls" when you most need it. You learn to push past the resistance that comes up with something hard.

Commit to two full weeks of one push activity to see changes in your mindset and energy levels.

The first week you are likely to have more resistance but keep reminding yourself that it is just one more day (each day for two weeks). This always makes me think of the "How Do You Eat an Elephant? - One Bite at a Time!" expression. Focus on the activity you are doing. Forget about how many days are left or even the long-term results you are aiming for.

When you are being your own Domme, you need a proverbial whip and a blanket. The whip is forcing yourself to take the action most needed to get the results you want in your business. The blanket is the kindness you show to yourself after you push through.

When a session ends, the submissive is often wrapped in a blanket and praised for being so strong, or good, or any other number of phrases they most need to hear. This allows them to integrate the experience and grow from it.

If you are going to Domme yourself, then you also need to give yourself that praise and encouragement. Wrap yourself up in a blanket of love and compassion so at the next session you are willing to surrender more, dig deeper, lean into that pain.

Your after-care blanket can be as simple as taking a moment to breathe in the joy of pushing through. Or you may make a note in your evidence journal – a notebook where you record all the evidence of the change you are asking for as a future reminder of your successes.

For example, recording the ways that more money is showing up or a sticker system of rewards for actions taken. This is one I love using.

I have different colours for different business activities, and each time I accomplish one, I put that coloured sticker on the calendar and acknowledge myself. It might sound silly, yet it appears we are still wired for sticker rewards. It offers the bonus of pushing you to get going again when you have a few empty calendar days.

Reality check: It is easy to share my good days and talk about the habits that work. But in the spirit of keeping it real here, there are days when I pull the bed covers over my head and sleep in an hour or two longer. There are days when I drive to the store for chocolate and eat my anxiety. There are also days when what I need to do is what I resist doing with the utmost vigour.

I no longer aim for perfection since that is unattainable. Instead, I strive for more productive days than unproductive days, and when I have a slump, I relax into that slump knowing that it is temporary.

What I have seen with myself and my clients is a slump only becomes an issue when I fight it and try to be both productive and a slacker at the same time. This leaves me feeling unfulfilled.

However, if I give in and allow myself an afternoon of popcorn and Netflix then 95% of the time the spring is back in my step the next day, and I look forward to getting back to work.

# Chapter 11

# THE BEAUTY OF SURRENDER

As a Dominatrix, there are two types of surrender you look for in your submissive. Each has its own rewards and unique experiences.

The first is the initial surrender of the need to be in control.

Often people who seek out a Dominatrix are engaged professionally in jobs requiring them to take charge, make all the decisions and hold a great deal of responsibility. This can create an imbalance, so they seek to re-balance through the relinquishing of power to the Domme. By letting go of controlling the flow and outcome of the scene, they surrender to her.

When you have a high-strung individual, who is always in charge, taking extreme measures really jars them out of "control mode." Sometimes, merely coming to the Dungeon - a space that exists out of the ordinary and appears utterly different from the rest of their life is enough.

Whether it is or not, the ritual of putting on a collar is powerful. It symbolizes the beginning of a scene in which the submissive has permission to let go. Over time this can become such a conditioned response that the moment the collar is in place, the person relaxes and surrenders.

If you are not into the Kink world, this type of conditioning can be attained through other rituals. Meditation done in the same space, seated the same way each time produces a similar effect, although more slowly, as it relies on you to be both student and teacher.

During the scene, the Dominatrix works to bring the submissive to this deeper surrender. For example, as she commands the submissive to crawl on his hands and knees, he physically offers his surrender as well as getting far out of his day-to-day life. He can let go and be present. This feeling of presence, while also increasing the discomfort of the tasks or pain consensually inflicted, drops him deeper and deeper into surrender.

This incredible space is where time stands still. Nothing else matters other than that very moment. The moment when the individual profoundly connects with their body is akin to many of the high-level spiritual-awakening practices.

In the Kink world, this is often referred to as "sub-space." Energetically, this is where time and space drop away with a complete surrender to the moment. By becoming fully present, all the troubles of the day that may have been in one's mind at the beginning disappear.

This creates a bond between the submissive and the Domme. As the submissive experiences this surrender with each scene, they are drawn more to the Domme, and the trust deepens with every meeting.

How would your business grow if your clients felt that deeply connected to you and your products or services? In business, creating a memorable experience for our clients is key to creating raving fans that keep coming back for more.

Taking a page out of the Dominatrix guide, there are things you can do to set up the "scene" for your clients that lets them know they are now in your trustworthy care. For each of you, it may look different but let me share how I set up the scene for my clients in business.

First, I create a space for people when they work with me. Think of it as a container of sorts. I energetically hold a space for each client where it is safe to surrender and transform what is longing to be changed.

There are also physical things, like starting each call with "wins" or sharing what is working well since so often their focus gets stuck on what is not working. The ritual of looking at wins first reinforces the positive changes that are happening and what is working.

If you look at interaction with your own clients, what do you do that lets your clients know you have their back? What rituals or practices do you use to show them you care deeply?

If you don't have any yet, then I invite you to play with what might be fun and helpful for your clients.

What would show them clearly you care about them and not just their money?

There is a little shop down the street from me that offers incredible vegan and vegetarian take out. The woman who runs the shop makes a point of getting to know her customer and what they do. Making you immediately feel welcomed and part of the tiny community she creates. She takes it a step further than that, if you arrive and there are other customers in the store, she will introduce you to the other customers and find a link between the two of you from what she has learned about each of you in the past.

On a larger scale, look at Starbucks, they implemented the system a few years ago where they ask for your name when they make you "your" special drink and call out your name instead of your drink to make you feel like you are part of the Starbucks family and build loyalty.

My accountant took me to lunch when I was facing bankruptcy and offered me advice and deep compassion that I would not expect from a "bean-counter" type, which has won my loyalty for many years since.

It is the little things that we do that show our customers that we care about them, and not just their money. Sending cards on their birthday is a nice touch, but what if you picked up the phone and called them on their birthday? How much more would that stand out?

## Surrender for the Domme

There is an exquisite joy in surrender. That joy explains why so many are drawn to return again and again to their Domme, to revel in the sweetness of complete and utter compliance. They experience moments where no pain, no crazy life, no problems exist. They genuinely become fully present.

You do not have to get into Kink and be a Domme yourself to experience this profound experience.

I have spent years teaching my clients how to connect with surrender energy for themselves. It is similar to a biofeedback system where I guide people to drop into their body. As they drop in, I scan them energetically to let them know what percentage they have surrendered or connected with their core.

At first, the process is slow as we deal with internal "gremlins" and their resistance to letting go of control. However, over time they begin to trust themselves and let go more and more. Imagine your best meditation session amplified tenfold.

When you dive into the pool of surrender energy, you connect with who you truly are at the core. That is a spiritual connection, no matter how you define it. The definition itself does not matter. Only the energy of "being" is important.

Spiritual connection is the feeling of ease amid chaos, a deep sense of knowing all is right in the world despite what is outwardly going on. For me, "being" is best described as a leaf floating along a gentle river without resistance, merely going with the flow.

Imagine for yourself what it feels like to be that leaf in the lazy river. Feel the ease in your body as you drop in deeper. Notice how the tension melts away, how your mind quiets and tunes into the stillness all around you. You could be in the middle of Times Square in New York City and still drop into this stillness if you allow your awareness to take you there.

Notice how it is about dropping in rather than pushing to find it. You yield to the connection to find the stillness. With practice, you can find this stillness even as you make haste to catch your plane or dash around the house to get the kids out the door in the morning.

The value of developing this practice is significant. Think about it. When you have those moments of brilliance or an idea which changes everything, what kind of mental space are you in? Were you rushing around like the proverbial chicken with its head cut off? I doubt it.

I would be willing to bet you were relaxed and optimistic. It is a mindset where you appreciate the weather no matter what the weather actually is.

That zone is where ideas take root. It does not happen when your head is cluttered and full of worry or fear. Instead, it happens when you connect with your playful, 5-year-old self who sees the world as a magical place.

I highly doubt this is new information to you. So, what stops you from making it important enough to put a daily practice in place?

Take a moment right here and right now to get honest with yourself.

What stories have you created that prevent you from connecting to that playful 5-year-old? Or, in other words, what stops you from developing a surrender energy that taps into your brilliance?

I suggest you write those stories down and reflect on them.

Now, ask yourself, "Am I willing to transform those old stories and the energy I have been using to keep them in place? Am I willing to rewrite the stories and turn them into something that allows me to relax and trust my own brilliance? Am I willing to have more brilliant ideas?"

Those old stories you tell yourself (your internal programs) get in the way of discovering surrender energy. You may need someone else to walk you through the process of letting them go.

Either way, take some time to reframe and change those stories. This is critical for you and your business.

The reframing technique is ideal for situations that are not highly emotion-charged for you. Write down how you see a particular event in your life.

For instance, "My husband drives me crazy when he talks to me from the other side of the house. He should know I can't hear him." A mildly annoying situation but not so emotionally charged that I would not be able to come up with a creative reframe.

To re-frame something like this, ask yourself, "If I were not upset by this how would I see this behaviour or situation?"

In the example, I could turn it around to "If it is important he will come to where I am to talk with me. Maybe I can let this go." Or "I can appreciate he is swamped and wants to keep communication with me going in our limited time together."

The reframe allows you to view the situation differently which will enable you to feel differently which, in turn, causes you to take a different action.

As I pointed out, this is NOT for situations in which the emotional reaction is intense (7+ on a scale of 10). In those cases, use a different approach or even better, work through it with someone you trust. You may need to look at what causes the reaction and do some work to clear out what it triggers in you. This is not work you can do objectively so a disinterested third party can help.

Meditation can also be a useful tool, not only for getting present to your body and the moment but also for releasing minor emotional upsets, so they do not build up in your system.

There have been countless studies done on the value of meditation and how many peak performers utilize mindfulness (aka surrender energy) as a daily practice. Most agree it significantly helped their business and of course, their health.

There are many methods to connect to surrender energy and to find ease in your body and with the world. You can release the need to fix or change any of it.

Keep in mind it is not about the "how" but more about adopting a practice that works for you. You can utilize guided meditations, mindful breathing (such as breathing in for a count of 4 and out for a count of 8) or a movement-based practice like yoga and tribal dance. Each of these examples is effective, so experiment with different options and see which fits your style best.

Find a method that allows you to move into surrender energy and utilize it every day. Invite in more of the ease of "being."

When I run workshops, we spend time learning to recognize this surrender energy, utilizing the breath and intentionally clearing out the crap. I teach you how to identify the baggage preventing you from connecting. I guide you to feel that surrender energy.

Learning those skills and experiencing that space is transformative for people. Surrender energy, the ability to let go, helps you notice and recognize the behaviours or choices not working for you. You can accomplish this without any force or hard work.

Surrender energy becomes effortless.

The more you allow yourself to surrender, the deeper you can go and perhaps even become your own Domme.

One way I guide my students to connect with this energy is to take something they 'struggle' with and imagine a line out in front of them. Try this yourself.

Imagine a long line out in front of you. This line represents a spectrum of the emotions you could have about something you are dealing with.

It can be thick or thin, coloured or not. You get to create and craft this so have fun with it. The more creative you allow yourself to be, the more you become immersed in the process, and the more dramatic the results will be.

Be sure to pick something small to experiment with, so you can do this without becoming overwhelmed. For our example here, let's say you feel shame about a mistake you made and are having trouble coming to terms with that shame.

First, let's take a deep breath. Everything is more comfortable with some oxygen in the body.

Now, imagine putting all your emotions about the situation onto the spectrum. One side holds the full intensity of your shame and all those judgements that go with it. The other side of the spectrum represents a space where you have a complete ease with the memory and zero judgements.

Now that you have emptied everything onto this spectrum allow yourself to move from one side to the other, noticing the sensations in your body as you do. No need to change or fix anything. Simply observe and notice.

Take your time. This is a process to be savoured, like fine wine. Sip it and roll it around to grasp all the flavours and sensations. No rush. Slide from one side to the other, back and forth a few times to get the fullness of this experience.

When you feel yourself easily move from one side to the other and really feel each side, drop in deeper to embrace the entire spectrum. All of it at once. No hiding from any part of it. You can move along that spectrum at will and by choice. Experience all of it.

This is surrender.

You are not fixing or changing any of it. You are not pushing anything away. You incorporate all of it and then make a choice of where you want to hang out without any judgement of good or bad. Purely a choice. At any time, you can sit in each part of the spectrum enjoying the flavours that the experience brings you.

This tool is incredible. It allows you to connect with the feeling of not being fucked up. By embracing the wholeness of who you are, you are not trying to change you or your feelings. You accept all of it.

In surrender, you find more options, not less.

Much like the submissive pushes past previously believed limits as a result of their submission, you will, too, if you practice surrender daily. Play with it and take it deeper when the time is right.

Naturally, I recommend working with someone who can hold the space for you to surrender because this can feel scary at first, like a foreign world without a map to guide or navigate. Having someone walk you through this process will deepen your practice significantly.

Learning to surrender to my body and my business has been an ongoing process for me. I work on it daily.

When I first explored the concept of the Inner Dominatrix, I thought I needed to show up strong and forceful in what might be called "push" energy. I attempted to bully clients into letting go of their shit and get moving with their business. While I got better results in comparison to traditional therapies, this layer of "push" energy did not help my clients or me to see the full depth of possible change.

Letting go of my agenda and holding an energetic space that respected their freedom allowed my clients to release their baggage and limitations with ease.

I was very fortunate to connect with Cristina, a fantastic woman I met through a group program. The course paired us up with two or three people to exchange sessions and move through the processes we were learning.

A gift in my life, Cristina helped me dismantle this "push" energy. She actually refused to let me work with her until I relaxed my energy and let go of my need to fix her. She helped me bring softness and surrender to the surface. This surrender energy took my work to a whole new level allowing me to deepen connections. I could hold a space, be softer and more effective by letting go of the "push" energy.

For example, instead of posting social media that had the feel of trying to corral or push people into working with me, I tapped into the playful detached (surrender) energy of being magnetic instead. And surprisingly, my sales doubled from that change. People reached out to have calls and to sign up for 1:1 programs.

Instead of pushing for people to let go, I hold the space for their change. I become an open invitation for them to move into seeing them as I see them. Understanding how incredibly powerful, talented and beautiful they really are, I let go of viewing them as needing to be fixed by these magical tools I possessed.

Change happens naturally when it is not forced on someone. By holding the energy open in a way that can't be ignored, my clients can't help but move toward it. Then the change happens on a deeper level. It's not for me. It's for them, and they find the inner strength they always possessed.

It is kind of like the Ruby Slippers. "You had the power all along!"

It sounds so easy on paper; just surrender.

Ha! When has surrender been modelled in your life?

I know that was indeed not part of my upbringing and not something I see very often with other people, particularly in the business world. So much of that world revolves around control and hustle with little talk about intuitive knowing or getting quiet in order to lead.

Those "push" people are loud and in your face. You sign up for their freebie, and next find your inbox filling up with emails from them telling you how much you NEED their program and how you are losing out if you say NO to them.

They have learned how to push all your fear buttons to get your money for their program. Some do mean well and help people, but the constant "push" leaves you with a bad taste.

I remember going to an introductory workshop for a system to help you sell to people based on what their buying styles were and learning to match them. It is not unlike the hundreds of classification systems available like DISC, Colors, Which Animal Are You, and so on.

I knew something about the system ahead of time because a friend of mine gave me an inside tour. I thought the content was interesting, perhaps a new spin on an old twist. Plus, this was someone I have great respect for. So, when the founder came to town and offered introductory training, I said yes and dragged a friend along with me.

Well, apparently this woman must have taken the "Sell From the Stage in a Slimy Manner" training before the event. She spent 45 minutes setting up the sale without offering much in the way of content. I felt she was completely out of integrity. After advising us against doing the "run to the back of the room" pushy sales, fifteen minutes later she offered a $20 item that was usually $100 but only available for the next 60 seconds for those who rushed to the front of the room.

My friend and I took that opportunity to get up and clear out instead of enduring any more of that aggressive sales pitch.

The speaker had a great system that could have sold on its own. There was no need for the intentional fear triggers and emotional button-pushing to generate sales. What a great lesson in just how ugly that approach is and how much of a turn off it can be for potential clients.

There are still times I get swept away with "push" energy or trying to do it 'right' and that voice in my emails and social media posts puts me out of alignment – kind of wonky – and it turns off my tribe.

It is so clear when I am on. People swarm around me, wanting more, longing to bask in that open energy. But when I am off, it's as if no one can hear or see me. I become invisible in plain sight. I am madly jumping up and down, yet to the rest of the room, I am a ghost.

## Daily Practice Options

## Go for a walk

Get out in nature and breathe in the energy of the plants, trees and animals that surround you. Walk slow enough that you actually feel the space around you. Do not walk to "just get it done."

## Meditation

There are many forms of meditation out there, so experiment to find one that works for you. Some people like to use a mantra, word or phrase to focus the mind while others enjoy listening to a guided meditation, so they have something to focus on.

## Breathing

The simple act of intentional breathing calms and centers your mind. A classic example is to exhale twice as long as you inhale, which has a physiological effect on your body, calming your nervous system.

## Drop into your heart

I teach my own daily practice to my clients, guiding them to sit still and imagine going into their heart and connecting with who they "truly be" at the core. From that space, I instruct them to radiate out gratitude and heart energy out to the whole world and beyond, going to the far reaches of the infinite space. You can linger for as long as you want with this. I recommend at least 5 full minutes daily for a fantastic reset.

# Chapter 12

# THERE IS NO ROOM FOR DOUBT IN THE DUNGEON

Fully clad in your leather corset and kickass boots, you step into the Dungeon to find your submissive waiting. Anticipation is palpable in the air as you stride across the room to him. The look you receive is one of hope.

Hope that you will be strong enough to break through any resistance so they can drop into the sweet surrender of sub-space. It is a look mixed with anticipatory fear. The kind of good fear that takes your breath away but does not let you turn away.

The Dungeon is no place for your doubts and worries. You don't get that luxury. You are called to leave them well behind to step into the role of the Dominatrix. You must hold the energy of one who is willing and ready to command and be obeyed.

Your submissive requires it, and your success depends on it. This may be a game, but it is a serious game, one that could have dire consequences if you let doubt and worry creep in to undermine your actions. Your attention must be focused on what you are doing, where you are striking, so you inflict the good pain and not cause damage.

There is another motivation for you to leave all that anxiety and uncertainty far behind. As you enter the Dungeon, it becomes a moving meditation for you as it is for the submissive. The energy feel is different, but there is a high from this dance that only happens if you are deeply engaged in the scene and utterly present to your submissive.

This is the energy component of the scene, the unspoken part of what is happening between the two of you. The movement of the whips creates a rhythmic trance for both of you. This is the spiritual component of the experience. The high is not just about feeling good but also transformation.

It transforms you, the Dominatrix.

This magical dance is not always achieved. It requires you to completely drop everything that exists outside of the Dungeon. You must let go of who you think you are and discover something else.

As you shed outdated ideas of who you are, you experience what you are capable of. Each scene takes your transformation higher if you surrender to the process, allowing the energy to mould you and move you.

If you step into your business with this same commitment to leave worries and doubts far behind, you will be unstoppable.

When challenges show up, you simply break out a larger whip and show it who is boss. You find creative solutions with ease and move past them with the precision of a ninja fighter.

It all starts with you!

You, unravelling your baggage. You, releasing those pesky self-judgements. You, choosing not to take on the energy and emotions of others. And you, showing up each day to dig in deeper and release more.

Then you back up that clearing work with some practical tools.

When doubt decides to raise its ugly head once again, you challenge that voice. You put that gremlin through the most fierce cross-examination process you can muster up. You ask the tough questions of the "Doubting Thomas" stealing the show in your brain. Part of the trick is attacking the voice as if it is outside of you and not part of you. Get into that role. Be that obnoxious cross-examining lawyer who wants to see the gremlin fall flat on its face.

It may say, "*Don't pick up that phone. They will just say No.*" You come back fighting with "**Have I ever died from someone saying No?**"

When it says "*You suck at creating marketing messages for social media,*" strike back with "**Did I walk the first time I tried it?**" or "**What is wrong with succeeding sloppily?**"

When it says "*This is not working. There is no money here. Go get a job,*" let the gremlin have it with "**Do you mean to tell me there is ABSOLUTELY no evidence to show that things are working? Have you even tried pulling your weight or are you simply throwing insults from the peanut gallery?**"

Have fun with this. Something incredible happens when we laugh.

Energetically, it breaks up the significance of a situation and gives your brain a chance to change gears and see things differently. This is often the opening you need to turn your thinking in a direction more aligned with where you are going.

On a physical level, a good laugh reduces the amount of stress hormones pumped into your body and gives your immune system a boost. Studies of laughter therapy on patients with dementia show some positive gains in the brain function as well. All in all, it's good news for us and even more reason to find the humour in our lives.

Changing an ingrained habit like doubt is not an overnight "Wave a Magic Wand" kind of exercise but rather, by sticking with it, you find things get easier. Easier to turn things around. Easier to see the fun in it for you. Easier to access the joy even while in the centre of a shit storm.

Follow the tools in this book. If you don't see the kind of change you want in the time frame you are looking for, then reach out to me, or someone like me to get things moving faster. We can rarely find our own crap to let it go. It almost always requires someone who is outside, looking in, to poke and prod until you surrender and let it go.

In the meantime, here is a fun visual to play with:

Imagine that your monkey mind – the one telling you all the reasons you will fail, or why you are not good enough – is actually your bratty submissive. Jumping up and down, just trying to get you riled up so that you will give him a stronger beating.

Put a ball gag on that monkey. Strap him to the chair and whip him a few times until he knows that you are CLEARLY in charge and the one running the fucking dungeon (your mind that is)!

# Chapter 13

## SEXUAL ENERGY

How strong is your desire? How passionate do you feel about life, your business, or your relationships?

The majority of people walk around half-dead, lacking any passion in their lives. Afraid to tune into their sexual energy, they deny their own desire for anything.

A friend of mine, Mary, runs this networking organization and she is a shining example of desire and passion. When she talks to you about her vision, it pulls you in, and you are compelled to say Yes to her latest venture.

Sexual energy flows through her and out to you as she tells you all about the event or meeting she is holding. She wraps you up in a cocoon of warm desire so inviting you must say Yes. I have felt it in action and watched her pull in others.

Because of this energy (plus a willingness to dig in and do the work of phone calls), she sells out her events. She creates a buzz. People want to be around her to become part of her dream.

Despite organizational challenges, she pulls in people to join her mission of opening chapters across the country. By the time this goes to print, she will likely be moving into other countries as well. Mary is a prime example of the power of unleashing your desire (energetically) on the world.

Like Mary, let people experience your passion for what you are creating.

I know from experience my tribe finds me irresistible. I have no need to push people into working with me. I show up with all of me, ramp up the sexual energy and they long to have what I am having. Even from across the room they palpably feel something drawing them in.

When I go out to networking events or to speak, I intentionally ramp up the sexual energy. It spills out from me and connects with everyone in the room willing to dance. This unspoken engagement is what attracts them. People find this energy irresistible and compelling.

It is one layer of how I intentionally show up authentically. It deserves more attention, as it has been left out for far too long in our businesses. Too many people confuse sexual energy with sexual acts and accept the idea it is inappropriate for the business world.

The thing is, when we leave out sexual energy, we also leave out the passion which pulls people and opportunities toward us. It's passion that excites people and makes them want to join our movement or cause.

That's why Mary is a good example. When she tells you about her next event, you feel inspired to join her because it touches your desire point. This is the place in you longing to feel alive and filled with passion, too. You can't help but say yes.

Mary delivers as well. She not only packs the house, but she attracts the most incredible sponsors. I can't think of an event she has done that did not include a wine sponsor -

which means free wine for the attendees and certainly adds to the excitement for people.

Let your sexual energy flow freely. It allows you to go out into the world and create your deepest desires. Sexual energy - not sex - is the engine fuelling our hearts and minds.

Our hearts are beautifully adapted to connect with others, to put the needs of the whole over individual needs and to feel present and peaceful.

Our minds are gifted at reason, logic, math and science. Helping us to map out a plan of action, they show us "how we get to where we want to go." Our minds create websites or search Google to find exactly what we are looking for. This is the beauty and power of the mind.

These two powerhouses are incredible, however without the fuel of our sexual energy they fail to bring things to fruition. With this fuel, we go out into the world and create our deepest desires. The heart without drive is lulled by your inaction, and the mind without motivation spins around, contemplating the many wondrous options of 'How.

By including our sexual energy, we add in the drive and internal motivation, so many of us try to find from outside ourselves.

Look to any Tony Robbins event. The vast majority in attendance are looking to him to supply their mojo. They feel temporarily pumped up and then crash days or weeks later.

Tony was right, he is not your Guru. You are!

When you tap the desire inside yourself, the fuel you need becomes available to rev up your engines and send you after your dreams, turning them into realities. Connected to your internal drive, you find that steady thrum of an engine that keeps you taking action for a lifetime, not just for a week.

For many years I ran my massage supply outlet from my mind. It dictated all my choices and directions. I made decisions based on what I thought would create the highest profit, using facts that seemed logical.

However, I lacked the desire for what I was creating. Truth be told, I was doing it for the money. I was sucked into the false belief that money would fuel my desire instead of the other way around. Despite this enormous obstacle, I managed to grow that business to a million dollars in sales.

However, I knew in my heart that my business was severely underearning and I was leaving vast amounts of money on the table. I knew I needed to go on the road and sell. I knew this because every person I spoke to bought more than they originally intended.

I was not devoid of sexual energy at this time, nor was I devoid of any passion, but looking back I was running on 10% of my capabilities. Even that 10% was enough to boost sales compared to most of the staff who had no sexual energy running.

I would resolve to "get out there and do sales calls," knowing it was required. I could see how it would work yet I could not bring myself to do the very thing that most needed to be done. My heart was not in that business. I was using it to run away from a crappy relationship and to save me financially.

Ha! If I had only known in those early days, the final outcome. I did not really want the business enough to do what needed to be done. I served clients from a place of service, but I would not go out to find those clients.

It is no wonder clients did not rush to spend their supply money with us. Many did business with us only because we were a considerable step up from the current supplier in customer service. But without the staff and myself fully engaging our compelling sexual energy, the customers left when something better showed up.

When they went somewhere else, I became resentful. I felt entitled to the business just because I wanted the money and I was there. Because of my own financial strain, I imagined they were obligated to shop in my store. This ugly and dark energy limited my business from thriving.

My focus on what was not coming in prevented me from shifting into gear to fix it. I never felt I could take the time. I had to run both the store and my massage practice. In those early days, I fully embraced "victim energy" and let me tell you, it was nasty ugly.

Looking back, I am not surprised that at one point the four full-time therapists working in my two massage clinics walked out at the same time. They did not feel loved or appreciated because I only saw them as money and felt entitled to it. I had a long list of reasons why they should feel grateful to me, yet I failed to see the flip side of that -- why I should feel thankful for them.

That lesson hurt.

They not only left but gave me notice on the very day I took the keys for a space twice our current size so we could provide a more beautiful, larger clinic. My rent doubled just as a good chunk of my base income disappeared.

Then my significant other at that time fuelled my fiery anger with my staff instead of helping me find a solution.

Attached to his own victim status, he validated my belief that I was right and they were wrong.

Looking back on it is painful.

I accepted whatever came along instead of looking for a great fit. I did that in my relationship at the time, and I did that in my business. Steeped in self-loathing, I rolled around in the "struggle" of life. I fed the angry victim inside, justifying her view that the world might be wonderful but not for her. Allowed to have just enough but never getting past the struggle, I believed I would never actually HAVE money.

Now I see this clearly. Hindsight is 20/20, after all.

I was not serving my clients, but instead, I attempted to be a rent-collecting lord, commanding them to do my bidding. Is it any wonder my business went bankrupt?

Let me be clear - I did care for the people who worked for me as well as my clients, but at the same time, this festering wound oozed, smelled and polluted my kindness. The moment there was the slightest "infraction" on the part of staff or customers, my rage triggered. Even when I was not voicing it, that energy was distinctly palpable.

As I reflect on those days, I have both compassion and regret for myself.

Compassion because today I understand how much healing was needed before I could be brutally honest about what I most wanted. Compassion because I could not see beyond my wounds to the people who tried to help. There were people in my life who believed in me, saw my pain and gave me space to be where I was at that time.

Today, I feel that same compassion for people who are where I was, struggling without realizing it has to do with who they are. Their underlying problems are not created by the environment, the economy or their families.

It takes courage to stare that kind of thing in the eyes and own it. Not many are willing to really see it. It is easier to blame others, and I know full well how tempting it is to stay there. I lived in my victimhood for 20 years before being willing to give up that identity.

The regret? Well, I let some of it remain as a gentle nudging for when I want to crawl back into bed and hide. There are still days when I prefer to binge watch something on Netflix than do what is required in my business. That regret reminds me of the lost sales, the lost time and reinforces my commitment not to repeat the past. I dig deeper into my passion for what I am creating.

That passion fuels my desire to succeed and moves me forward. Getting the "right does" can be a tricky balancing act. Too much and I curl up on the couch. Too little and I slide into believing it won't matter if I don't take action. I can convince myself to watch just one more episode on Netflix or paint my toenails before writing another chapter.

## Success Story

I can still remember sitting there with my feet in a hot tub under the full moon in New Orleans having, what I originally thought, was a casual conversation with girlfriends. Asking questions, giving answers, being open and honest about things I'm not normally so open about; money & sex. Dana's gifts are so natural that it was just a part of the conversation. She simply asked me to get out of my own damn head and tap into my sexual energy

"Ask the question, Kelly and then FEEL the answer. What makes your sexual energy turn on?"

"$87,000."

To which Dana asked, "$87,000 total or $87,000 per month?"

INSTANT buzz of energy from deep within as she answerd, "per month."

That type of physical response is not something you forget, nor is it something that I could deny.

A few short months after that I was doing month end paperwork and I realized, "OMG! This was a $69,000 month! I'm WELL on the path to what Dana helped me uncover a few short months ago!!!" I was completely floored.

In a conversation between friends she had created a space that was safe, open and honest and allowed me to let down my walls and get down to my truth. She allowed me to see what I truly desire and what turns me on. I really don't think I could ever thank her enough for teaching me how to use Sexual Energy as a tool for manifesting what I want in my life.

~ Kelly Grignon ~ *www.kellygrignon.com*

**Engaging the Sexual Energy**

So, how exactly does one engage the sexual energy?

*****

**Warning**: If you have sexual trauma you have not dealt with, please leave this alone for the moment and come back to it later. There is a high probability these exercises will trigger old memories and emotions from your past.

---

Working through them alone is not the kindest route to take for you and your body.

In these exercises, it's likely the 'go it alone' route will be the least effective since our natural tendency is to repress and push these feelings back down instead of facing them head-on. Find someone who is highly skilled in this area to move you through it safely and effectively.

Change does not necessarily require years of therapy. In fact, if you have already done some work, it may only take a few sessions to see dramatic changes. It depends mainly on how much has already been cleared out and what remains in your system.

You are aiming to reclaim your ability to feel safe again. That is better accomplished with help.

*****

Now that you are ready let's make an agreement to move through this slowly. There is no rushing things here. Take your time and really savour the process. Get to know the energy. Imagine you are dating and learning all about this new energy. How it feels. How it moves. What it is like to dance with it.

Perhaps this will be your first time connecting to your sexual energy, or maybe you are well-versed in this area. Either way, relax and give yourself permission to let it be what it will be.

**Level 1**

Go out and buy yourself some underwear that feels sexy.

This may seem like a contradiction after stating it is not about sex, but stay with me. This purchase is only for you. We can learn from the women in France who love to purchase beautiful undergarments just for themselves. It is not about showing off for their partner but rather a secret pleasure to enjoy as they go about their day, knowing that under their regular clothes they wear something beautiful.

So go shopping just for you! Do something beautiful and sensual that makes you feel good.

This engages the sexual energy. You will be more aware of your body and the pelvic floor, which is the storehouse of this energy. Tune in and turn it up.

Wearing pheromones is the other tool you can play with, purchased online or through your favourite sex aid supplier. Perhaps they do what they say, or maybe it is only a placebo. Either way, they make you aware of your own sexual energy and help many people at the beginning of this journey.

Not unlike training wheels, while learning to ride your bike, you don't really need them. But if you falter a bit, it sure is nice to have them there to keep you upright.

One of my friends swears by pheromones. As a waitress, she experimented with them. On the nights she put them on (a dab behind each ear), she saw about a 40% increase in tips. She never told anyone, but that small dab gave her a boost in confidence which undoubtedly her customers felt. She felt sexy and confident, and they responded with a more generous tip.

Not a bad investment for a $15 bottle.

## Level 2

Now you are ready to connect with the power source of your sexual energy which sits in the pelvic floor. If you look at the pelvis and imagine it to be a bowl, a container for the power you draw on when you need refuelling.

To get started, close your eyes and shift your focus to the pelvic floor. Take your time to drop in and just sit there for a bit. Just be in that energy, not changing it or influencing it in any way. Simply be there.

Notice.

Notice the energy. Notice how it is different from elsewhere. Notice the hum.

There is a tendency with my clients to want to move on from this quickly. They feel like they are not 'doing' anything. They prefer to push forward. They want to get to the "good stuff."

This is the good stuff.

When you surrender to this energy, you surrender to your power and learn to harness it. Move into being instead of doing.

When you master experiencing this energy without the need to 'do,' stress slips away, and the pressure you put on yourself falls off. Mastering this gives you freedom and power so take your time.

Sit with it for much longer than you think you need.

Each breath, dropping in more.

Set a timer and practice this for 15 minutes each day. Extend the time when you are ready for more bliss. It is a type of meditation without the need to still the mind. You are merely breathing and noticing. That is all.

**Level 3**

After you have taken time to intimately connect with your sexual energy, you are ready to play with this energy. Invite it to move up your spine and out into all the cells in your body. If you are a more kinesthetic person, try rocking your pelvis backward and forward to move the energy.

Remember that energy follows intention so all you need to do here is to invite the energy to flow and it will. If you are not feeling it move then, you may have some internal resistance to allowing your sexual energy to move freely.

Most commonly this is repressed sexual trauma. If this is part of your history and it has not been thoroughly dealt with then consider working with a trained professional.

Once you have a good grasp on moving the energy through your body, it is time to have some fun and take this out into the world. Engage with unsuspecting people who are unaware of what you are doing.

I love sending my clients out to coffee shops to witness the reaction of people when they walk in with this energy in full swing. Heads turn to watch them.

When I have done this, strangers have assumed I am famous and ask for my autograph. Too funny! Of course, I played along and signed their napkin. Perhaps they were trying to pick me up but no matter. It was super fun.

Networking events are also a playground for me. As I mentioned earlier, I intentionally ramp this energy up. Men and women are drawn to me, wanting to talk with me. This is much more fun than the old way of going to these events.

Experiment on your own. Notice what shows up for you and of course, have fun with it. This is meant to be a delightful exercise.

Take this energy with you on stage, on sales calls, negotiations, asking for upgrades, while creating sales copy.

Take it anywhere you would like people to feel delighted to offer you money or perks.

Engaging your sexual energy will trigger them to unconsciously reconnect with their own desire and juiced up to move forward in their life, too. Even if it is just in that moment, they will be grateful you showed up, and they had a chance to connect with you.

In fact, this magnetism can be so intense you may find yourself receiving unwanted attention or attracting clingy people. Not to worry. The more you own your Inner Dominatrix, the easier it will be for you to lovingly tell them to fuck off and have them look forward to the trip.

# Chapter 14

# STRAP ON YOUR BOOTS

Every good Domme has a few pair of killer boots to strike fear and anticipation into her subs. Those incredible boots that look so good they are often the focal point of promo pictures for those in the Pro-Domme world.

It seems only fitting we pay tribute to The Boots in this book.

After all, many a submissive has taken a turn licking the boots of their Mistress, humbly paying respect and demonstrating their willingness to serve.

As an entrepreneur, The Boots are the physical representation that you mean business, that you are going to stand your ground. You are not to be pushed around or bullied into deals that are not favourable to you as well as to them.

You need your boots. Trust me. There are going to be many times when customers, staff and suppliers will want to use you to their advantage. You have to put your foot down in a way that says, "Yes, I care. No, you may not walk on me."

Am I saying you literally need to wear boots?

Hardly! You can be just as powerful in a pair of runners as your power pumps. It is never about the costume but about who you allow yourself to be in that costume. Those proverbial boots change your physical stance thus transitioning your inner state to root you firmly in the energy of the Dominatrix.

Having a great outfit is a tremendous asset. It connects you to your Inner Dominatrix and says to the world "I am here. Get on board or get out of the way!" It supports the power mindset for negotiations, presentations, sales calls or networking.

Granted, in the world of the Dominatrix is the expectation there will be some sort of a costume to intensify the overall experience. However, showing up in the boardroom or at a sales presentation with kick-ass boots might work against what you are trying to accomplish. Opting for appropriate attire that boosts your confident energy will achieve what you are looking for.

Take a look at your current wardrobe. Identify your power outfits and footwear so you can quickly call them into action when needed. In fact, while you are there, pitch out anything you do not feel great in. It is high time you allowed yourself to look and feel your best, even if you are wearing yoga pants. Merely get the yoga pants that feel fantastic and fit you perfectly.

In the beginning, having a power suit with power shoes can be the vehicle for connecting to that Dominatrix energy you are looking to bring into your business. In time, you will be able to pull out that energy even in your pyjamas.

However, it's not only about the proverbial boots and clothes.

Along with a great power outfit, you are going to need some energy-shifting routines to jazz up your body and rev up your engines just before that important meeting or presentation. Look for quick tools you can quickly call on, regardless of where you are.

If you have watched the movie "I am not your Guru" with Tony Robbins, then you know he has several mental and emotional shifting routines he utilizes just before getting on stage. His energy level is precisely what he requires for being in front of a large audience.

First, he makes sure his team is taking care of things so that he can take a few moments to focus. One tool he uses that stood out for me was his mini trampoline to get the blood flowing and energy pumped up.

For the rest of us who don't have a team, you need to figure out how to separate from the day-to-day chaos of life to get your head in the game. Just as the Dominatrix is required to leave the rest of the world at the dungeon door, so too, we must separate mentally to focus on what we most need to accomplish.

Getting your head in the game means regularly clearing out the baggage of the past, disconnecting from other people and releasing the self-judgements. Use the Blast-it tool explained earlier to move out any 'negative' energy you have about yourself. Use it to get rid of those interesting stories you make up about how good you could be or will never be. Blast any energetic judgements you may be subconsciously taking on from others. Imagine pulling it all out. Take a deep breath and blast all that crap.

When you make this a regular routine, there is less and less you need to leave at the door before entering your business since you will have cleared it already. At this point, a simple intention of expanding your energy field out will allow you to unplug from the craziness of the world. Some call this energy field your aura, or your chi. It is the energy aspect of who you are and can extend way beyond your physical body. You can be fully present and bring your entire mental, emotional and intuitive capacities to the table.

For a simple but effective self-clearing tool feel free to jump over to the website and grab this download. www.innerdominatrix.com

Here are a few more simple tools that work well:

Deep breathing is absolutely the most versatile and portable tool. Taking a deep breath is highly effective at resetting your nervous system. In fact, taking a few deep breaths moves your body out of the "flight or fight" response and engages the relaxation response.

Important tip: The more deeply engaged you are in "flight or fight," the more deep breathing will be required to shift things back to a relaxation response. This is the physiological state your body engages to calm the nervous system, slow the breathing, and create a feeling of ease. However deep the "flight or fight" response is, keep going. At worst your body will receive more oxygen. At best you will feel more at ease.

Beyond the basic of breathing, our posture also profoundly impacts us.

I am grateful for the excellent research on the effect of standing in a "power pose" to change your emotional and energetic state.

The two most popular I have found are the "Wonder Woman" pose and the V-pose.

You create the "Wonder Woman" pose by placing your fists on your hips and standing tall with your feet slightly more than hip-width apart. Take a few deep breaths and feel the energy rush. Even just thinking about standing like this, you can feel the energy pulse in your body.

I love recommending this one before "battle "because it creates the state of readiness to stand up for what you want.

Heading off to negotiate a deal? Stop off in the washroom and hold this pose for a few breaths and see what shifts.

The V-pose is very similar only this time, with your arms above your head and out in a V, and your feet hip-width apart, take a few deep breaths in and out. Notice the difference in energy with this pose compared to the Wonder Woman pose.

This one is fantastic for revving up the juices for presentations, talks, or even sales calls.

These poses will not create a permanent change to your confidence. They are a booster – a lift to get you through those more challenging events. You are still going to need to address and clear the underlying programmed thoughts and beliefs which keep you seeing yourself as less than others or not enough.

# Chapter 15

# THE TOPPING HIGH

There is an incredible energetic high that comes from a good session with a submissive. As they drop into 'sub-space,' there is a 'topping-high' that often happens for the Domme/Dom/Dominatrix at the same time. The rhythmic sounds and the dance-like flow of the scene create a hypnotic trance for both players, although it plays out differently for each. The bottom/submissive can perceive it as weighty, a loss of control that feels heavenly, being supported and having no need to do or be. For the Domme, it is often more like a peaceful rush, simultaneously feeling a heightened awareness while being entirely at ease in the world.

Having played on both sides of the whip I had an extra connection with my submissives, knowing the sweetness of the surrender and the complete melting into the space that is all things and nothing. I easily felt when they were dropping, and as they dropped, I allowed myself to go deeper into the energy flow. The dance played out, as if by sub-titles. A melting of the two energies into this oneness created a singular entity in the play between us.

Losing a sense of oneself, experiencing a spiritual connection can only come when both players drop into the energy, facilitated by the pain for the submissive and by the physical challenge for the Domme. Each pushing past what they saw as limitations before the session, they discover new strengths and new highs as a result.

Time and reality seem to disappear, and you melt into the nothingness of all that is. This is a state of consciousness that many who practice meditation for decades begin to tap into. Dropping off the need and necessity of anything in this world. They experience a total freedom in letting go of everything.

The more you let go of the judgements (all of them), the more you can experience this incredible space in your day to day life. You can tap into this high of the Dominatrix when you allow yourself to slip into that space between, the space that is all things and nothing at the same time.

If you are holding on to things being 'right' or 'wrong,' you will not find that space. It is like trying to relax into a hammock (the surrender) while at the same time clinging to the tree (your judgements). Doing both at the same time is impossible. If you want to experience the bliss of the hammock, you must risk letting go of everything else.

The reward is great, and, while our resistance may feel very real and justified, in the end, is merely an illusion and not real at all.

You can also tap into this 'topping-high' in your daily life, by allowing yourself to be engrossed in the moment. But how often are you doing one thing and also thinking of what you are going to do next, or what you forgot to do yesterday?

This is your moment to drop in, to let your current surroundings and what you are doing hold ALL of your attention.

It has been scientifically proven we are not capable of multi-tasking. Yet the fear of missing out or feeling overwhelmed keeps most of us looping around in this crazy pattern of being highly ineffective and unable to experience the joy of being fully present. We miss the hyper-alert and highly creative state that comes from being singularly focused.

Why is it so hard? If the reward is great and results are improved, why do we generally not choose that focus?

Allow yourself to notice what happens when you start to shift from the scattered un-focused to being present. What shows up? Resistance? Are the gremlins jumping up and down?

The 'unsafe' alarms start going off because we become aware of the things we had been avoiding, such as feeling 'not good enough,' 'not smart enough' or other bullshit rolling around in your brain. They all pop up with a vengeance, and you feel the anxiety of all of them all at once.

The thing is, the more you use the tools I shared to blast them out, breathe through them or even allow yourself to see how false they actually are, the quicker you move past that anxiety and drop in to 'being.

**Tool**

When you find yourself in one of these whirlwinds of low-grade anxiety and unable to be singularly focused, take out your phone and set an alarm for 30 seconds.

For 30 seconds, place your hand over your heart area and breathe.

Allow yourself to follow your breath in and out. With each exhale, let yourself expand out more and release the hold anxiety has on you. Visualize this anxiety as it clings on to you. As you breathe and expand, it has less and less to grab hold of. Observe it sliding off of you.

Now, breathe and feel your energy connect with the core of the planet. Feel yourself supported by the earth while also expanding your energy out to infinite spaciousness.

This process allows you to feel everywhere while also staying firmly connected to the here and now.

Placing your hand on your heart is a quick method for bringing your attention to that area and dropping into your body.

# Chapter 16

# "After Care"

As the dungeon scene concludes, the submissive is tenderly released from all the restraints. Gently removing the handcuffs, ankle cuffs and anything else attached to their body, allows them to ease back into normal movement after an hour or two of the scene. The toys are set aside for cleaning later. The time for the after-care begins.

The warm nurturing side of the Dominatrix comes out with a chance to be kind and gentle, honouring the submissive and the courage they showed during the session. After all, they worked just as hard as you and have done so well to surrender to you completely.

You wrap your submissive in a warm blanket and tend to them with water or food while they integrate the session. Here is the space where you acknowledge their strength and praise their bravery and how they did something they thought they could not.

It is not uncommon for the submissive to have the "shakes" as muscles release tension and their body releases trauma - not from the session but from the past. Old wounds and hurts from years gone by gently shake out as the submissive rests.

In this space, they are at their most vulnerable. They need compassion and kindness to balance out the harshness of the scene and set things right in the world once again. Grounded and present in the moment, this is the time for them to relax and be soothed. You help them ease back slowly to the "reality" around them, cognizant of their surroundings and how they now fit into the world.

The learning and transformation from the scene have yet to be formulated into words. It will be a while before the submissive articulates all that happened in the session. There will be time for a de-brief later that day or maybe in a day or two. Now it is enough just to BE.

Be still. Be connected. Be surrounded by love.

I remember from my days playing on the submissive side, how sweet the sound was of my Dom saying, "You were such a good girl." It seemed like music to my ears.

I craved that delicious praise for pushing through and surrendering. The impact of those words at a time of complete and utter exposure released the pain of the trauma of my childhood. It also set up a desire to push further the next time, knowing that at the end would be that sweet praise, my reward for the pain along with the bliss of utter surrender.

It seems crazy a phrase which, outside of that context would be condescending and annoying, turns out to be just the words needed to create the healing I was longing for. But then the whole world of Kink is a kind of upside-down paradox that delights, allures and draws you back, again and again.

This part of the scene is often missing from the Hollywood portrayal of Kink. They love to show you the lashings and degradation, but they fail to take you through to the end where things are put right in the world for the submissive, so they can stand taller than they did before.

In my time in the Kink community, I saw a range of after-care styles. Some would wrap up their submissive and cocoon them for hours allowing them to linger as long as their hearts desired while others were dropped off like packages and forgotten, left in the hands of fellow submissives to be tended to.

I suspect that the dominants who pushed off the care to others had not healed their own wounds. Giving someone else what we have not yet experienced is rare.

While Kink offers a resource for healing your body and your mind, not all who participate in BDSM do so for the growth. Many are in it just for their own perverted pleasure and do not care about the submissive to whom they are doling out tortures.

There are also submissives to match them. They are not looking for compassion but to relive abuse and reinforce their belief that this is what they deserve. Perhaps they are aware of this pattern, or maybe they act it out subconsciously. The why does not matter, only that we are aware not everyone has the same motivation. This is true in business as well.

I love the lines from the famous Eurhythmics' song, Sweet Dreams about how some people like to be used, and some like to do the using.

This is valuable knowledge so you can easily navigate around people uninterested in your best interests. Be aware of those looking to use you as a stepping stone as they climb up. You can learn to identify them while being devoid of the need to make them wrong. Merely step around them and carry on with your plan.

Granted, this is not always easy. You want support in place to remind you and pull you back on track quickly. As your business grows, that support becomes invaluable to you as a person as well as to your bank account. You want someone on your side to call you on your bullshit or when you are in danger of being swept up by someone looking to take advantage of you. This lovingly honest person will be the most valuable person on your team, as your coach or among your friends.

There is an abundance of "placaters" on this planet already. Instead, look for those unique individuals who dare to be honest with you. You want someone who risks your wrath to speak up and say what most needs to be said. You need the ones who calmly share with you when you are not right.

Being in business will push you to your limits and beyond. Just when you think you are about to break, something gives, and the tide finally turns. Take some time for kindness after you go through your times of torture. And trust me there will be days that physical torture would seem easier to endure. When you come through to the other side of it, have after-care set up to lock in your learning. Be ever so gentle with yourself.

What would your caring Domme suggest? How do you tend to your emotional bruises? Do you see those hurts in the way that a submissive cherishes their marks as a reminder of sweet surrender and leaning in to feel their own strength?

Make a list of the things that replenish you at the soul level. Book a massage. Read a book. Listen to a podcast. Go for a walk out in nature.

When you have come out the other side, and your nerves are as jagged as coral, refer to your list and pick something just for you.

Stop, breath, and tend to your wounds with care and compassion. Pushing for more is going to get you less, and you will not be replenished for the next challenge.

I wish you much success in your business but most especially that your business turns you into the kind of person you have been longing to become.

# Appendix – The Tools

Welcome to the easy reference for the tools that are mentioned in this book. Some will be an expansion from the chapters, and most are pulled in as a handy, all-in-one place to refer back to again and again.

Also make sure to stop by www.innerdominatrix.com for more resources deeper explanations of the tools.

**Expanding Out!**

This continues to be my foundational tool in all my work and the one tool that has turned my exceptional empathy abilities from a crippling handicap to the secret superpower in my coaching work.

This prevents you from taking on the energy of others in the first place, allowing you to have ease as you move about the world.

**How to:** Allow yourself to take a deep breath, and playfully use these questions to move your energy field out further and further, creating more and more space for you and your body.

I wonder what it would feel like if I was to expand out as big as this room?

I wonder what it would feel like if I was to expand out as big as this country?

I wonder what it would feel like if I was to expand out as big this planet?

I wonder what it would feel like if I was to expand out as big this solar system?

I wonder what it would feel like if I was to expand out as big as this galaxy?

I wonder what it would feel like if I was to expand out as big as this universe?

I wonder what it would feel like if I was to expand out to infinite space?

For a deeper understanding and audio explanation listen to this Inner Dominatrix podcast episode http://www.danapharant.com/ep57

## Putting it into regular Practice

Link the expansion to something you do everyday, many times a day, like going to the bathroom or taking a drink of something.

The other option is to train yourself by setting an alarm that chimes every 30 minutes. You want to train your energetic muscles to be expanded out ALL the time so that you can get the full benefit of this tool. It may take up to a year to really lock it in, but it only takes the length of one exhale to make it work so keep the reminders up.

The Key - Utilizing questions to gain new awareness or insight

When you are asking a question, imagine you have no idea of what the answer is. Drop into a place of deep curiosity and ask it of the Universe. Then WAIT for the answer.

Go back to having fun and trust that at some point you will get the inspiration or idea that answers your question.

**Challenge your need for control with questions like:**

"Will this actually matter in 5 years?"

"How could this turn out better if I let go of control?"

# Clearing the Judgement aka charge/resistance

We create an energetic imprint or 'charge' in our system when we align ourselves with a judgement - deciding things are black/white; right/wrong.

Clearing out the charge or energy imprint requires merely two elements – connecting with it (which is often feeling the charge or noticing it in some manner) than choosing to let it move out of your system.

The majority of people have not had enough experience with the act of letting go, so having a tool to work with is a simple and effective method until you "get" that it works because of your choice to let it go.

There are a plethora of tools that fit the 'psycho-energetic' realm. Some are complicated while some are simple, but they all work only to the degree you are willing to trust and let them work.

Here are my top picks to get started with. Each one begins the same – with you tuning in to the energy of the item you would like to move out.

Then use one of the following:

**The Breath**

Take a deep breath and imagine releasing all the stuck energy from your body. It may be letting it release from your feet by imagining it to be like pulling the drain on the bathtub. Or merely allow it escape through all the pores in your body.

Send the energy out to be recycled.

**Blast it Out**

This is one that can be fun to play with.

Imagine pulling out all the energy associated with whatever it is you have tuned into. Put it all in a big pile in front of you and then blast it with an energy bomb that annihilates the crap you wish to release.

Have fun with some sound effects with this one and engage your body in the whole process. This will likely get you laughing, which assists the movement of this energy out of your system.

# Intuition Bootcamp Training

First, you need to get familiar with your energetic compass. This compass tells you what is true or yes for you and what is false or no for you.

Sway Test

Stand with your feet hip-width apart. Say out loud "Body, show me a yes." Notice the direction of movement that indicates yes.

Then say "Body, show me a no," again noting the direction that indicates no.

Now, you are ready to use your body as a pendulum, asking it yes or no questions. Please refrain from fortune-telling type questions. That shit does not work. And yes, I have tried asking for the lottery numbers.

**Muscle Testing**

This is similar to the sway test in that you are asking for a yes/no response, only you use the finger and thumb of one hand held together with comfortable pressure, like an "okay" signal. Insert the finger and thumb of the other hand into the circle created and pull against them, as though to pull open the loop. Generally, 'yes' holds strong, and 'no' opens.

You may need to play with this to lock in the trust of your body's intuitive knowing to your cognitive brain.

**Light vs Heavy**

This variation is a more advanced tool for intuitive knowing. However, the application is more versatile since you can gauge how much of a 'yes' or 'no' something is. This is helpful in comparison type evaluations.

Make a statement you know to be true like "I am an infinite being" or "My name is {your name} and notice the reaction in your body. How does it show you a 'light' sensation?

Then make a contradictory statement that you know is false like "I am a limited piece of crap." Again, notice the feeling in your body of 'heavy.'

**The Training**

Start with simple choices that don't matter. Should I wear this or this?

Then put on the item that your intuition said yes to or felt lighter. Don't think about it, just follow it.

Keep looking for all the little choices you can make in your daily life to build your intuitive knowing and following.

As you get stronger at this, start to play with questions like "What will my life be like in 5 years if I do (option A)?" Gauge how light or expansive that response is. Then ask "What will my life be like in 5 years if I do (option B)?" Again, gauge that response and follow the one that feels lighter. No thinking, just follow it.

If they happen to feel equally light, pick either and go. If they are the same it is just a personal choice, so choose and move on. Remember you are also practicing to be decisive.

**What to do when you have multiple choices?**

When you want to use your intuition in areas such as networking events to "see" who to connect with, or when you have a multitude of choices, like ordering off a menu, play with this tool.

Allow your gaze to go slightly out of focus and see the whole area or list of choices at once. With the intention of allowing your intuition to light up the best one for you, you will notice that one person or one item suddenly comes into focus.

In the case of the networking event, go and talk to them, don't think about it just do it. If you are in a restaurant, close the menu and order the item that lit up.

# Success Stories!

*Hey Dana!*

*Okay, so I've been taking Intuition Boot Camp seriously and doing the damn thing. Holy fuck... I didn't realize how much my limitation was 'snuffing out' my higher self. All the second guessing and back and forth. It's feeling so freeing, making a decision and sticking with it.*

*I've made a powerful decision that no matter what I choose, it will all work out and the Universe is supporting me. I realize where I was projecting human relationships onto the Universe. Like, if I behave in the "right" way then I'll be rewarded and good. I've been projecting this dynamic onto the Universe providing me with money. I've decided that no matter WHAT I do, I'll be financially supported. It takes the charge off my decisions and allows me to make them purely from what my heart, soul and pussy desire. There's no "getting it right." I get to be supported financially and in ALL ways because I fucking do.*

*I've been using muscle testing to help make decisions. Squeezing my thumb and pointer finger together, asking myself a question and trying to pull them apart. Then asking the opposite and pulling apart again. When my fingers stay tight, that's the answer. Trusting the motherfucking wisdom of my body.*

*I've been high flying these past few days and staying focused on keeping my mind aligned with my vision. The how isn't up to me. It's also a desire to live all of my life in this way, of trusting what I can't see yet unfolding. It's not about getting from point A to point B and then I'm golden. It's about learning to live in the possibility of uncertainty all the time. Because... everything is always working out for me.*

*Thank you!*

*Kat Trimarco*          *www.kattrimarco.com*

# How Can This be Fun?

Lean into the things you currently see as painful or uncomfortable and let yourself find ways to make it fun. If nothing comes to you, then lean into the 'pain' and discover the joy of overcoming this challenge.

You can always try out that cold shower trick.    (I know you are longing to try that one out. LOL)

# Surrender - Daily Practice Options

Go for a walk.

Get out in nature and breathe in the energy of all the plants, trees and animals that surround you. Walk slow enough that you actually feel the space around you. Do not walk to "just get it done."

Meditation.

There are many forms of meditation out there, so experiment to find one that works for you. Some people like to use a mantra, word or phrase to focus the mind while others enjoy listening to a guided meditation, so they have something to focus on.

Breathing.

The simple act of intentional breathing calms and centers your mind. A classic example is to exhale twice as long as you inhale, which has a physiological effect on your body, calming your nervous system.

Drop into your heart!

I teach my own daily practice to my clients, guiding them to sit still and imagine going into their heart and connecting with who they "truly be" at the core. From that space, I instruct them to radiate out their gratitude and heart energy out to the whole world and beyond, going to the far reaches of the infinite space. You can linger for as long as you want with this. I recommend at least 5 full minutes daily for a fantastic reset.

# Dominate Your Monkey Mind!

Take charge of that negative chatter in your mind by challenging the lies it is spewing.

Even better, put a ball gag on him and toss him in a cage just for fun!

# Engaging The Sexual Energy

## Level 1

Go out and buy yourself some underwear that feels sexy. Do something beautiful and sensual that makes you feel good. This engages the sexual energy. You will be more aware of your body and the pelvic floor, which is the storehouse of this energy. Tune in and turn it up.

Wearing pheromones is the other tool you can play with, purchased online or through your favourite sex aid supplier. Perhaps they do what they say, or maybe it is only a placebo. Either way, knowing you are wearing them makes you aware of your own sexual energy. This practice helps many people at the beginning of this journey.

## Level 2

Now you are ready to connect with the power source of your sexual energy which sits in the pelvic floor. If you look at the pelvis and imagine it to be a bowl, you see a container for the power you can draw on when you need refuelling.

To get started, close your eyes and shift your focus to the pelvic floor. Take your time to drop in and just sit there for a bit. Just be in that energy, not changing it or influencing it in any way. Simply be there. Notice the energy. Notice how it is different from elsewhere. Notice the hum.

Set a timer and practice this for 15 minutes each day. Extend this time when you are ready for more bliss. It is a type of meditation without the need to still the mind. You are merely breathing and noticing. That is all.

## Level 3

After you have taken time to intimately connect with your sexual energy, you are ready to play with this energy. Invite it to move up your spine and out into all the cells in your body. If you are a more kinesthetic person, try rocking your pelvis backward and forward to move the energy.

Remember that energy follows intention. All you need to do is invite the energy to flow and it will. Once you have a good grasp on moving the energy through your body, it is time to have some fun and take this out into the world. Engage with unsuspecting people who are unaware of what you are doing.

Take this energy with you on stage, on sales calls, negotiations, asking for upgrades, while creating sales copy. Basically, anywhere you would like people to feel delighted to offer you money or perks. Engaging your sexual energy will trigger them to unconsciously reconnect with their own desire and feel juiced up to move forward in their life, too.

Even if it is just in that moment, they will be grateful you showed up, and they had a chance to connect with you.

In fact, this magnetism can be so intense you may find yourself receiving unwanted attention or attracting clingy people. Not to worry. The more you own your Inner Dominatrix, the easier it will be for you to lovingly tell them to fuck off and have them look forward to the trip.

## What is Your 'After Care' Routine?

Take a moment to jot down what replenishes you. Refer to this list on those days when your head is firmly up your ass.

# About the Author

A self professed workaholic who will make time for wine with friends or a ride on the motorbike with her husband, Dana is committed to doing business as a spiritual practice and being a warrior of consciousness.

She is not afraid to tell you the truth, and dive deep into the shadow aspects of life and our egos to explore new truths, new concepts, constantly growing and changing as years go by.

Living in Barrie, Ontario Canada she gets to enjoy the full range of the seasons offered, although truth be told, summer is by far her favorite.

She is happiest leading a workshop or speaking on the stage or simply soaking up the energy of the land without the need to do anything in particular.

**Next Steps**

Get on the list for updates, workshops and more content from Dana – www.innerdominatrix.com

We would LOVE to hear how this book helped you in your life or business!

Email: dana@danapharant.com

**Join the group:**

https://rcbrand.ly/InnerDominatrixGroup

Book Dana for your group, or hosted retreat feel free to email dana@danapharant.com